Praise for *Cultivating Deeper Connections in a Lonely World*

Personal. Encouraging. Soul-searching. Biblical. If you've ever felt lonely or unconnected, longing for deeper, more intimate and fulfilling relationships with others, don't miss this book. Becky Harling offers well-researched and practical strategies for developing meaningful and in-depth friendships. First, read this book on your own. Then gather a small group of people who want to be intentional about studying and implementing the transformational action steps Becky offers as you commit to developing deeper connections with God and others.
CAROL KENT, Founder and Executive Director of Speak Up Ministries, speaker, and author, *Speak Up with Confidence*

Becky Harling shines a light on the loneliness epidemic, masterfully offering practical and biblical wisdom to heal our lonely, isolated, and yearning spirits. From the first page, she extends grace, kindness, and biblical balms of truth. As a professional in full-time Christian ministry and a single mother, this book spoke to my situation, encouraged much-needed self-reflection, and presented practical steps toward fulfilling relationships and authentic dependence on Jesus. A must-read!
JENN SCHECK, Sr. Vice President of Human Resources, Focus on the Family

We all know what loneliness feels like, but not many know what to do about it. Becky Harling helps us discover how to feel a sense of connectedness and belonging in a very isolating world. She shows us how to develop community that links not only hands, but hearts for a lifetime.
SHARON JAYNES, bestselling author of *When You Don't Like Your Story: What If Your Worst Chapters Could Become Your Greatest Victories?*

Becky Harling says it best: *loneliness is not the absence of people—it's feeling disconnected from those people.* This wonderful book helps us rediscover the biblical attitudes we need to form meaningful connections with others. Readers will love the prayers and questions at the end of each chapter for deeper connection with God, themselves, and others. As you read this book, you'll grow in humility, empathy, and kindness—the foundation of authentic connection. By the end, you'll feel motivated to foster deep friendships where you cheer one another on, rather than living in envy or judgment. This book is a treasure!
HEATHER HOLLEMAN, speaker and author of *The Six Conversations: Pathways to Connecting in an Age of Isolation and Incivility*

Becky Harling's *Cultivating Deeper Connections in a Lonely World* lives up to its title, for Becky doesn't just throw out scriptural truths, but also puts meat on those good bones with her captivating illustrations, providing a model to enrich and solidify our relationships.

DEE BRESTIN, author of *The Friendships of Women* and *Idol Lies*

Loneliness according to the surgeon general is at an all-time high. Many cannot name even three close friends. In this profound book, Becky shows us how to take the initiative to create closer friendships so we never have to feel alone.

GEORGIA SHAFFER, professional certified coach, PA licensed psychologist and author of *Taking Out Your Emotional Trash*

If you've been struggling with feeling lonely, Becky Harling is the friend and wise guide you need. She will come alongside you as an encouraging sister, speak truth your heart needs, and give you practical steps to finding the connections your soul truly craves.

HOLLEY GERTH, *Wall Street Journal* bestselling author of *What Your Heart Needs for the Hard Days* and *The Powerful Purpose of Introverts*

With biblical wisdom, practical insights and compassionate advice, Becky Harling gives us a road map out of loneliness into the deeper connection we all long for.

PAM FARREL, author or coauthor of 61 books, including bestselling *Men Are Like Waffles, Women Are Like Spaghetti* and *Glimpse of God's Glory*

I found my heartbeat in Becky Harling's new book, *Cultivating Deeper Connections in a Lonely World*. I immediately thought, *This is a writer who knows what my life is like!* Because I work from home, I often feel isolated, lonely, and physically disconnected from others. Becky's challenges to be vulnerable, less critical, and less sensitive to others' offenses spoke to me. This is a much-needed resource for individuals, church groups, and even the business world. Relationships matter. They cultivate meaning for our lives and effectively help us live out our faith. I highly recommend this book.

JANET HOLM MCHENRY, author of 27 books, including the bestselling *Prayer Walk* and her newest, *Praying Personalities*

Don't read this book if you don't want to take a long hard look at yourself and the things that keep you from connecting with others. Don't read this book if you don't want to learn how to submit your life, preferences, and circumstances to Scripture. Finally, don't read this book if you want to stay lonely or disconnected. For those who do want deeper friendships, practical tips on how to transform your relationships, and an internal shake up, this book is for YOU! Becky Harling has done it again. She's after heart change, radical obedience, and passionate love for God and others. She's after the things that could possibly change our social structure as we know it. If you also want those things, read this book!

TABI UPTON, author, speaker, and cohost of *Mornings with Tom and Tabi*, Moody Radio Chattanooga

CULTIVATING DEEPER CONNECTIONS

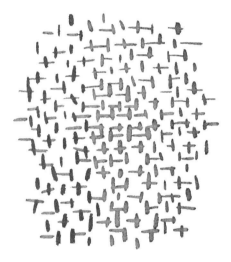

in a

LONELY WORLD

BECKY HARLING

MOODY PUBLISHERS
CHICAGO

Published in association with the literary agency of The Blythe Daniel Agency, Inc., P. O. Box 64197 Colorado Springs, CO 80962-4197

Edited by Pamela Joy Pugh
Interior design: Ragont Design
Cover design: Brittany Schrock
Cover concrete texture copyright © 2024 rawpixel.com/Freepik. All rights reserved.
Author photo: Ashlee Kay Weaver

Library of Congress Cataloging-in-Publication Data

Names: Harling, Becky, 1957- author.
Title: Cultivating deeper connections in a lonely world / by Becky Harling.
Description: 1. | Chicago, IL : Moody Publishers, [2024] | Includes
   bibliographical references. | Summary: "Loneliness is an epidemic, but
   you can live life with a deep sense of belonging. Becky taps into the
   deep ache of loneliness and shares with readers a rich theology of
   belonging. We don't have to live isolated and unconnected. In fact, we
   mustn't. Our souls were designed for more"-- Provided by publisher.
Identifiers: LCCN 2024010776 (print) | LCCN 2024010777 (ebook) | ISBN
   9780802430939 (paperback) | ISBN 9780802473356 (ebook)
Subjects: LCSH: Loneliness--Religious aspects--Christianity. |
   Fellowship--Religious aspects--Christianity. | BISAC: RELIGION /
   Christian Living / Personal Growth | RELIGION / Christian Living /
   General
Classification: LCC BV4911 .H37 2024 (print) | LCC BV4911 (ebook) | DDC
   248.8/6--dc23/eng/20240331
LC record available at https://lccn.loc.gov/2024010776
LC ebook record available at https://lccn.loc.gov/2024010777

Originally delivered by fleets of horse-drawn wagons, the affordable paperbacks from D. L. Moody's publishing house resourced the church and served everyday people. Now, after more than 125 years of publishing and ministry, Moody Publishers' mission remains the same— even if our delivery systems have changed a bit. For more information on other books (and resources) created from a biblical perspective, go to www.moodypublishers.com or write to:

Moody Publishers
820 N. LaSalle Boulevard
Chicago, IL 60610

1 3 5 7 9 10 8 6 4 2

Printed in the United States of America

This book is lovingly dedicated to my two dear friends:

Jill Geldmacher and Judy Dunagan

Both of you have journeyed alongside me for many years.

You've been faithful and loyal during
some of the darkest hours of my life.

And you've celebrated every victory with me.

I am so thankful for you;
for the times, we've cried, prayed, and laughed.

I treasure my friendship with you both and consider myself
blessed with two of the dearest friends a person could have!

I love you both!

Contents

1. When You Don't Feel Connected *9*

2. Embrace Humility *27*

3. Let Go of a Critical Spirit *43*

4. Develop Loyalty *61*

5. Start Cheering, Stop Comparing *77*

6. Be Attentive *95*

7. Offer and Receive Comfort *111*

8. Open Your Heart *and* Your Home *129*

9. Don't Be Easily Offended *147*

10. Find Your Prayer People *163*

Afterword *177*

Acknowledgments *179*

Notes *181*

CHAPTER ONE

When You Don't Feel Connected

Encourage one another and build each other up.

1 Thessalonians 5:11

We are wired to connect. Neuroscience has discovered that our brain's very design makes it sociable, inexorably drawn into an intimate brain-to-brain linkup whenever we engage with another person.

Daniel Goleman

My husband, Steve, and I arrived home after some intense weeks of ministry. I was exhausted and a bit cranky from traveling through so many different time zones. We had been with people round the clock and I'm an extrovert, so I should have felt elated.

Instead, I felt drained. I love meeting people and I had met plenty. However, my soul felt dry, completely parched. As I reflected on what was going on inside, I felt shocked to discover a deep ache of loneliness in my soul. How in the world could I feel lonely when I had just spent countless hours with people?! As I analyzed my feelings, I realized I was longing for deep connection. I needed extended time with God and my people.

Though I had ministered for God, I felt disconnected from Him. I longed to nestle down for extended time in His loving presence. I wanted to experience the joy of being fully known and loved. Even though I had ministered with my husband for weeks, we hadn't had "us" time. I felt disconnected from him too. On top of all that, I missed my kids, grandkids, and close friends. While we had been with lots of people nonstop, I lacked deep connection.

I missed the people who knew me best.

The morning after we arrived home, I got up early and brought all my jumbled feelings before the Lord. As I knelt in His presence, I began to realize that while ministry had been exciting and exhilarating, I was longing for more. Not more events. Not more flights. Not more opportunities. I was longing for deeper connection. I needed unhurried time with God, Steve, my family, and friends! Each of those relationships are precious to me and yet, because of ministry demands, each had in some way been neglected.

> **Loneliness is not the absence of people—it's feeling disconnected from those people.**

You've felt the ache of loneliness from time to time as well. After all, it's why you picked up this book. Loneliness can hit you at the most unexpected times. Perhaps the job is going awesome and in many ways you're climbing the corporate ladder, but then it hits you how many of your relationships have been sacrificed on the altar of success. Or you've been busy chasing toddlers, and you realize it's been weeks since you've had adult conversation and connection with friends. Maybe you attend a megachurch, but you really don't have close relationships there. When Sunday morning rolls around, you don't feel excited about attending.

The truth is our hearts were created for connection. Loneliness is not the absence of people—it's feeling disconnected from those people.

All of us, whether introverted or extroverted, need close, deeply connected relationships. It's the way we were created. We crave a place of belonging. When there is a lack of significant attachment, feelings of being isolated settle in. Loneliness doesn't imply a lack of friends. It means we don't feel connected.

At one time or another every one of us has felt lonely.

It's the ache of the mom with young children craving adult conversation.

It's the cry of the single woman longing for a spouse.

It's the throb of the married woman longing for deeper intimacy.

It's the sting in the heart of the woman who feels uninvited.

It's the misery of the one who's been divorced.

It's the agony of the widow whose husband is gone.

When we feel lonely it's a signal that we need to return to what we were created for: deeply connected relationships. And according to recent research, loneliness is at an all-time high.

LONGING FOR CONNECTION

A public statement from the surgeon general of the United States revealed that one in two adults feels significantly isolated. The report suggests that loneliness is the new epidemic and that we now have a dire need to again figure out community and what it means.[1] In other words people are feeling disconnected. That number is staggering and interestingly, it didn't stem from the COVID pandemic of several years ago. Many have called the pandemic the great revealer. It didn't cause the problem but definitely showed us how deep the problem is. Our loneliness has been growing steadily over recent years.

Maybe you've felt lonely after a divorce, or when moving to a new city, or after a conflict with a friend. You might feel lonely because you're single and you've been praying for a mate for years. On the other hand, it could be that you are married but feel like you and your spouse are on different planets. Perhaps you've grown too busy. Long hours at work are preventing you from enjoying deep conversation with your family and friends. It's possible you've been hurt, and as a result you've built sturdy walls of protection around your heart. Unfortunately, those walls have kept other people out and now you are feeling all alone. While the reasons are many and varied, we are now facing the epidemic of loneliness.

Eve accepted a new job, a great career opportunity in management she couldn't pass up, but she's having a hard time connecting with her new coworkers. It seems that everyone else has been with the small company for years, and she keenly feels she's an outsider.

Noelle has moved to a new area and is considering trying to meet new friends online but isn't sure that's a good idea. Week after week goes by as she hesitates, and now she feels stuck in a pattern of unwanted solitude.

Roberta is single but would like to meet someone special to share her life with. When she returns to her apartment every evening after work, she feels depressed and wishes someone were there to greet her and ask about her day.

Candy is married, but the distance she feels in her marriage leaves her feeling isolated and sad.

You may look at your pastor or someone else who seems to be a people person and projects an aura of being upbeat. However, even ministers and others in positions of leadership experience feelings of isolation on a regular basis. The demands and pressures, not to mention the criticism, can leave many feeling like they don't have a friend in the world. Author Ruth Haley Barton writes about the loneliness that leaders feel: "On some days the magnitude of the responsibility and the awareness of our aloneness can be crushing."[2]

While some may have lots of connections on social media, those aren't necessarily true connections. In fact, research shows that people who spend long hours on social media are more lonely than ever.[3] Social media serves a function; however, it is not a replacement for authentic close relationships.

Honestly, loneliness is a frequent visitor in our broken world, and we're grappling with a profound sense of disconnect. To make matters worse, our loneliness is costing us not just emotionally but also physically. The CDC links social isolation and loneliness to depression, anxiety, type 2 diabetes, heart disease, stroke, dementia, and more.[4]

Though these reports are challenging, loneliness is nothing new.

LONELINESS IN THE SCRIPTURES

As we read the Scriptures, we discover that many heroes of our faith felt lonely:

- Moses felt the loneliness of leadership. With deep fear of abandonment Moses cries out, "If your presence does not go with me, I don't want to go at all!" (Ex. 33:12, 14; my paraphrase).

- Job felt lonely when his friends brought him no comfort and instead kept accusing him of sinning against God (Job 4–23).

- Nehemiah felt lonely as he led the wall reconstruction project (Neh. 2:16).

- Elijah felt lonely in the cave and cried out, "I am the only one left" (1 Kings 19:10).

- David felt lonely as he hid from his own son who was trying to take his life (Ps. 3).

- And ultimately, Jesus our Savior felt lonely in the Garden of Gethsemane the night before He was going to die, when His friends kept falling asleep instead of praying with Him (Matt. 26:40).

Here's the thing: if you wrestle with loneliness, let go of the guilt because the guilt isn't helping you. It's normal to experience seasons of loneliness, as I described above. However, it is not meant to be the general tenor of our lives. Instead, our daily life needs to be anchored in a deep sense of community, an intimate relationship with God, and close attachment with others.

The truth is, all of us desire genuine, loving, connected relationships. We want to feel like we belong and that we're known and loved. We need each other. And you know what? That's God's desire for you as well.

THE THEOLOGY OF BELONGING

The desire to connect is from God. Our souls throb with a hunger that only God Himself can heal. He created us with that divinely given ache to connect and, amazingly, God Himself aches for us. Shocking, I know! God yearns for us to have a deep relationship with Him. He is the only one who can fill the deepest longing of our hearts.

Author Ruth Myers said it this way: "God offers us a perfect and permanent love, a love relationship that can meet our deepest needs at every point of life and forever."[5] Only as we enjoy secure attachment to God are we able to love others out of the overflow of a full heart. For the record, that is exactly God's plan! He never created us to live our lives in isolation. Rather, He created us for intimate relationship with Him and others. He designed us with a need for community and connection.

Way back in the beginning of the Scriptures, God said, "Let us make mankind in our image" (Gen. 1:26). Just as God lives in eternal community between Father, Son, and Holy Spirit, so He designed us for community. After He made man, He said, "It is not good for the man to be alone" (Gen. 2:18). In other words, because man was created in God's image, he was designed for community. Shortly after God created the man, He gave him a

> *The more firmly rooted we are in Christ's deep love, the more willing we will be to love and connect with others.*

15

friend, partner, and soul mate in the person of Eve. It's clear that God doesn't want us to live in isolation—He designed us for relationship both with Him and others.

On the night before He was crucified, Jesus prayed, "I have given them the glory that you gave me, that they may be one as we are one—I in them and you in me—so that they may be brought to complete unity. Then the world will know that you sent me and have loved them even as you have loved me" (John 17:22–23).

The deeper and more intimate our relationship is with God, the more at home we will become with ourselves, and the richer our connections will be with others. Too often our relationship with Jesus is, in the words of one writer, "seriously underdeveloped."[6] As a result, we are not able to offer deep friendship and connection to others. Tight bonds of community form out of the overflow of a heart that has experienced deep belonging in Christ.

Jesus yearned for us to understand the depth of our attachment to Him. Before He ascended into heaven, He had some comforting words for His disciples, and I believe His words can bring us comfort for today as well. He told His disciples not to feel troubled or worried, but to trust Him. He went on to say, "I will ask the Father and he will give you another advocate to help you and be with you forever—the Spirit of truth. The world cannot accept him, because it neither sees him nor knows him. But you know him, for he lives with you and will be in you. I will not leave you as orphans; I will come to you" (John 14:16–18).

Did you catch that? Jesus promised He will not leave you as if you were an orphan. He won't abandon you! He left you the Holy Spirit who would be your 24/7 journey mate. As a result, **you are never alone!**

I remember how God brought His tangible presence home to me in a very personal way when I had cancer. I was in the hospital hooked up to all manner of machines after having a six-hour surgery to remove both my breasts. Steve, my husband, and I had decided beforehand that after the surgery was complete, he would go home and be with the kids. We knew they were terrified over the fact that I had cancer.

However, when Steve left to go home, I felt afraid and lonely. I knew he had to leave, but I didn't want him to go. I felt so alone and vulnerable. Someone had given me a little teddy bear that was created for those battling breast cancer, and I remember in the darkness of my room holding that teddy bear and reminding myself of the words I had learned as a child, "Never will I leave you; never will I forsake you" (Heb. 13:5).

In the darkness of my hospital room with machines beeping I felt the Lord speak in comforting whispers, "Becky, I am here with you." Before I fell back asleep, I silently acknowledged His presence with heartfelt gratitude, "Thank You, Lord Jesus, that I can trust Your promise. You are here with me. Never will You leave me and never will You forsake me. Not even during cancer. I relax in Your presence, knowing You are with me and in me."

You see, my friend, that's where our path out of loneliness begins: our relationship and intimate belonging with Christ. Once we have received His love by faith, we are bonded with Him. He will never leave us nor forsake us. Not during a divorce. Not when work deadlines pile up. Not during cancer or other illness. Not during wars or persecution. Not during earthquakes. Not during hurricanes. Not ever! He is Immanuel—God with us. He is faithful, and you can trust Him to keep His word. The Spirit of Christ lives in you (Gal. 2:20). You never have to worry about being alone again!

Out of that securely bonded relationship we are then able to reach out to enjoy rich relationships with others and find healing from loneliness.

WHERE DO WE GO FROM HERE?

In this book, we will consider tangible stepping stones to deepen your relationship with others. We're going to answer the question: When you don't feel connected, what can you do? As you read, keep in mind how you can change the narrative and take initiative.

You might consider yourself a victim of loneliness. In your mind, you rehearse messages like "I'm not a good conversationalist" or "I never get invited because I'm single" or "I'm just not good at relationships."

I suggest that you change the narrative. Remind yourself that you have deep value, and that God calls you precious. He has designed you to be a gift to others. Beyond changing the narrative, start to take initiative. Invite a friend to coffee. If you feel shy, plan questions you can ask to get to know the other person better. Or call someone on the phone, and simply ask them how they are doing and what's new in their life. One psychologist suggests calling at least three friends per week. That's a great start. Join a community group at your church or reach out to some of your neighbors. The thing is, in order to have friends, you must put in a little effort.

Through the rest of the book, you will find very practical steps you can take to triumph over loneliness. You won't be able to develop deep relationships with everyone. That's not possible or healthy, but as you continue reading, you'll discover tips for how to strengthen your relationships so that you have several close-knit connections with whom you feel a sense of secure belonging.

The Bible will be our authority on relationships. We'll study the principles of deep connection as taught in the "one another" statements found in the New Testament. Each of these statements teaches us a quality that needs to be found in our relationships. So if you don't feel connected, and you're feeling a bit isolated, here are some practical steps you can take that we'll be unpacking throughout this book:

Embrace Humility
Let Go of a Critical Spirit
Develop Loyalty
Start Cheering, Stop Comparing
Be Attentive
Offer and Receive Comfort
Open Your Heart *and* Your Home
Don't Be Easily Offended
Find Your Prayer People

At the end of every chapter is a section called ***Digging Deeper into Connection***. This section will include some reflective questions to consider under Deeper Connection with God, Deeper Connection with Yourself, and Deeper Connection with Others. At the end of each chapter will also be a brief section reminding you of how God exemplifies each of these characteristics in His friendship with you. The Bible is the place where we discover who God is, so I've added some verses in this section to give you a true picture of what an amazing friend God is to you.

As we discover the beauty of one another and allow the Word of God to teach us how to enjoy rich relationships, both with Him and others, we'll find ourselves feeling less lonely. Instead, we'll enjoy tight knit community and intimate connection. Are you ready? Let's dive into deeper connection together. Why not pause now, before you read any further, and pray this prayer with me?

> *Lord Jesus, You know my ache to belong. Thank You that You created me to have a desire to feel connected both to You and others. As I embark on this journey, I pray that You would allow me to feel Your love and enjoy Your presence. Thank You that Your Word teaches me that You have loved me with everlasting love and You have drawn me to Yourself with cords that can't be broken by anyone or anything. Thank You that nothing can separate me from Your love. Show me the beauty of living in relationship with others as You have outlined in Your Word (Jer. 31:3; Rom. 8:38–39).*

DIGGING DEEPER
INTO CONNECTION

Deeper Connection with God

1. *When you consider connecting more deeply with God, what comes to mind?*

2. *One of the primary ways we connect with God is through the Bible. That may feel overwhelming to you. But if you look at Scripture in bite-size pieces, it will feel easier.*

3. *Look up the following verses and consider what they teach you about the relationship God wants you to enjoy with Him.*

   Jeremiah 31:3
   John 15:4–6
   James 4:8

   What did you learn about God from each of these verses?

4. *Another way we connect with God is through prayer. When we pray, we can talk with God about anything that is on our hearts. He is always willing to bend down and listen. How have you viewed prayer in the past? How might it change your relationship with God to view prayer as simply a conversation with God?*

Deeper Connection with Yourself

If you feel disconnected with yourself, you can't enjoy deep friendships with others. One way to connect with yourself is to spend time in solitude so you can understand yourself more fully. Neuroscience seems to point to the fact that if we understand ourselves more deeply, we are able to connect more effectively with others.[7] Spend a few minutes considering:

1. *Do you feel comfortable when spending an hour or two alone? Why, or why not?*

2. *When do you feel the closest to God? How do you best experience His presence?*

3. *What are your hopes and dreams as you read this book?*

4. *When have you felt disappointed in friendships?*

5. *What qualities do you offer friends that could bless them and help them feel connected to you?*

6. *God was intentional in the way He created you. What are some unique gifts that God has given you?*

Deeper Connection with Others

1. *Out of your friends, who do you feel the closest to in this season of life?*

2. *Who do you feel distant from and why?*

3. *Who in your life could you share a deep problem with and not feel judged?*

This week, go to the store and pick out a card for a friend. Write a short paragraph affirming some qualities you see in their lives that bless you. Get a stamp, address the card, and send it! In this day and age of texting and emojis, people appreciate the beauty of a handwritten note.

God Longs for Deep Connection with You

"I have loved you with an everlasting love; I have drawn you with unfailing kindness" (Jer. 31:3).

"The LORD your God is with you, the Mighty Warrior who saves. He will take great delight in you; in his love he will no longer rebuke you, but will rejoice over you with singing" (Zeph. 3:17).

"Greater love has no one than this: to lay down one's life for one's friends. You are my friends if you do what I command" (John 15:13–14).

"See what love the Father has lavished on us, that we should be called children of God!" (1 John 3:1).

"This is how God showed his love among us; He sent his one and only Son into the world that we might live through him. This is love: not that we loved God, but that he loved us and sent his Son as an atoning sacrifice for our sins" (1 John 4:9–10).

COURTNEY'S STORY

Courtney and her husband, Jake, had a desire to serve sacrificially. So they became licensed as foster parents. They cared for their kids' practical needs, loved them, and prayed over them. But the journey had been tough. While she was trying to make a difference in this dark world, Courtney felt isolated and alone.

Recognizing that they desperately needed community, Courtney and Jake began coming to our church, and there they found connection. People stepped up and offered to help where needed. Courtney and Jake found a place to belong where they would feel valued for what they are doing to help kiddos in the foster care system. Courtney often asked for prayer.

Courtney knows she cannot do this journey alone; while she and Jake are partners in this ministry of childcare, the fact remains that he works full-time, so the daily responsibilities are largely hers. She needs others as part of her support team. She has been humble enough to reach out to our church community for help with diapers, clothes, food, and other essential supplies.

The journey to take in foster care kids is a very lonely one, and at times those feelings can be overwhelming. However, Courtney serves with a loving, joy-filled heart. Recently, one of her friends described Courtney to me as one of the most humble, unassuming people she knows. Yet Courtney is aware of what she can and can't do. As she serves, sometimes in lonely places, she knows she needs others on the journey with her.

CHAPTER TWO

Embrace Humility

Clothe yourselves with humility toward one another.

1 Peter 5:1b

---

*The true way and the sure way to friendship is through humility—
being open to each other, accepting each other just as we are,
knowing each other.*

Mother Teresa

Not long ago, I read something that caught my eye: "People who are more humble tend to step up to help others more than people who tend toward arrogance."[1] The article went on to make the case that humble people make the best friends. I agree.

Tracy is a great example of this. She is the mama of three young boys, and she runs a nonprofit that serves underprivileged children. However, beyond all that, Tracy is an amazing friend. She humbly serves each Sunday at church. She often brings meals to young families who have sick children or are struggling in some other way. She consistently offers to help and encourage. In addition, Tracy is an amazing listener. I have watched as others pour out their hearts to her. She listens attentively, gives fabulous hugs, and rarely brings the focus back to herself. It's not that she's not vulnerable. She does make herself vulnerable, she just doesn't scramble and shout for attention. You know what? Tracy is less likely to feel lonely, because everyone wants to be Tracy's friend! As she humbly gives herself to others, she enjoys deep relationships.

My pastor, Andrew Arndt, and his wife, Mandi, demonstrate humility in their leadership. When Steve and I went out to lunch with them recently, they asked us, "How did you navigate the teen years with your kids?" Though they are strong leaders, they are willing to ask and receive input from others. What a beautiful quality! In his profound book *Streams in the Wasteland*, Andrew wrote, "We need wise, thoughtful, deep, honest community. Community that can hold the emerging faith of young adults, the many difficulties associated with marriage and family and work, the doubts and questions of the saints as they arise and as they (often) become more pronounced over the years—without hitting the panic button. Community that offers an open heart."[2]

Humility encourages vulnerability, which results in honest community.

As we stated in chapter 1, God designed us for community. When we received Christ as Savior we were invited into belonging, not only with God but also with His family. Tucked within this sacred invitation of belonging is the sacred call to humility.

THE CALL TO HUMILITY

While our Western culture may value independence, nowhere will you find independence affirmed by God in the Scriptures. Quite the opposite. God continually calls us to community and interdependence. Living in relationship with others is how we best develop the godly quality of humility. When we enjoy life together, we realize we are limited, and we realize our own opinions are not the only way to think of an issue or situation. We have to bend and compromise, but the result is beautiful.

As you embrace humility, you become a better friend and your friendships are more authentic.

The apostle Peter, addressing a community of believers living in Asia Minor, wrote, "Clothe yourselves with humility toward one another, because, 'God opposes the proud but shows favor to the humble'" (1 Peter 5:5). At the time Peter wrote this, "Slaves wore a particular garment that showed their role and status. When they tied on their white *enkomboma*, they were reminded of their station."[3] Peter was reminding believers to put on the clothes of a servant and to live unpretentiously in all relationships.

Similarly, the apostle Paul wrote to the believers living in Philippi that they were to "in humility value others above yourselves" (Phil. 2:3b). Paul goes on to write, "In your relationships with one another, have the same mindset as Christ Jesus" (v. 5). Paul explains in vivid detail exactly what the attitude of Christ looked like. Take a moment to read Philippians 2:6–11.

Now you might be wondering: What exactly are we talking about when we talk about humility? And how does it strengthen our relationships and make us less lonely? I'm so glad you asked!

WHAT IS THIS QUALITY CALLED HUMILITY?

Here's how I define humility:

> Humility is having a true understanding of yourself
> and being willing to serve others.

Let me see if I can describe this a bit more. The person who is humble knows their strengths and weaknesses. They are comfortable in their own humanness. They are able to serve and sacrifice on behalf of others. In their friendships, they focus on the interests of others rather than always needing to be the center of attention. They are secure serving others and even asking for help and advice.

The Crossway prayer journal *30 Days on Humility* describes it this way: "A posture of the heart and mind characterized by the absence of pride and self-importance and a commitment to the well-being of others."[4] I like that definition as well because it includes our hearts and minds.

As I think about Jesus and His humility, His wasn't self-deprecating. He knew who He was and why He had come. As a result, He felt no need to grasp for power. He knew He already possessed the power that came from being the Son of God. He lived within the limitations of a human body confined to a twenty-four-hour day. Though He was the King of kings, He served others and lived out His life in humble obedience to the Father.

WHAT DO HUMBLE PEOPLE DO?

Listen Attentively

While there are many skills that contribute to humility in friendship, this is perhaps one of the greatest. It takes quite a bit of humility to lay aside your thoughts and completely focus on another. Those who have a humble view of themselves don't interrupt or dive in with their own story or give advice. They don't show up as the truth police, correcting the thoughts of others. They simply concentrate on drawing the other person out and remain curious through the entire conversation. They live as though on a quest to discover the treasures buried in another's story.

Serve and Encourage

Like Courtney and Tracy, humble people are willing to step into the darkness and serve. They make or buy a meal for someone who is sick and demonstrate a willingness to serve or help in other ways as well, setting up chairs for a corporate meeting, babysitting to give a caretaker a break, or running errands for those older who are housebound. They put on humility and remind themselves that they are called to be servants.

My friend Lynda is like this. She and her husband, Bruce, both in their eighties, are two of the most humble people I know. They serve dinner each week at the Friday evening service hosted by our church. In addition, Lynda faithfully texts and encourages those who need prayer. She greets at the door on Sunday mornings and is the first to ask how you are and how she can pray for you. She is a beautiful example of a humble friend who is willing to serve and encourage others.

Apologize

All of us are wrong at one time or another. All of us offend others or say thoughtless things or make mistakes in our friendships. All of us overreact to things or become easily offended. The key is to be able to say, "I'm sorry. Will you forgive me?"

Recently, I read a story about Abba Agathon, one of the early church Desert Fathers. He's been quoted as saying, "I tried never to go to sleep while I kept a grievance against anyone. Nor did I let anyone go to sleep while he had a grievance against me."[5] In other words, not only did Abba Agathon keep his heart free from grudges against others, but he also quickly asked forgiveness from others whom he might have offended so that they too could sleep in peace.

I've been trying to practice this at night before I go to sleep. Using the technique known as the Examen, I prayerfully think back through my day. I ask forgiveness for anything I've done or any person I might have offended. I let go of any feelings of anger or resentment toward anyone who might have hurt me that day as well. In this way, when I lie down to sleep at night, I know I have asked Christ to clean the slate of my heart. He then helps me sleep in peace and wake up ready to love others again.

May I ask you two uncomfortable questions? When was the last time you admitted to a friend that you were wrong? And when was the last time you asked for someone's forgiveness?

Be Authentic

Here's where many of us run into trouble. Perhaps because we've been hurt in friendship before, we build protective walls around our hearts. We show up with our friends as though we have life all together because we believe that's safer. I mean we don't want them to know we might be struggling with fear, or anxiety, or self-doubt, or grief, or any other perceived negative emotion. We want them to see our together, confident, makeup-on type of self. But here's the thing. That's not your most authentic self—that's you pretending. And wow, that's a whole lot of pressure! Why not just be you? Lay aside your perfect self, and you know what? You might just discover others like you more when they know you're not perfect.

Now you might be thinking, "Well, that all sounds great Becky, but how do I change so that I develop a heart of humility that spills naturally into my friendships with others?" Great question! I'm so glad you asked.

EMBRACE YOUR LIMITS

Humility begins when we embrace our limits. All of us have limitations, and yet particularly here in Western culture we chafe against them. We want to become more! Often life coaches tell us to move beyond our self-limiting beliefs and to strive to become all. I understand their emphasis on not succumbing to a belief system that demoralizes us.

However, the truth is all of us actually do have limitations designed by God for our lives. When you think about the great sin of Satan, the fallen angel, what was it? It was the quest to become more! As a result, Satan's heart was taken over by pride and God kicked him out of heaven (Ezek. 28:16). Of all the sins we could possibly commit, pride seems to be the worst in God's eyes. The way to not give arrogance any kind of foothold in your life is to continually embrace your limitations. This doesn't mean to be self-deprecating. It means you will abide by the limitations God has given you: physical, emotional, and spiritual.

Pastor and counselor Pete Scazzero offers this wise counsel: "Limits are God's gifts to us."[6] Scazzero goes on to say that when we break the limits God has placed on us, we enter the enemy's territory. Think about it. In the garden, Satan tempted Adam and Eve to break the limit God gave when He instructed them not to eat from the tree of the knowledge of good and evil (Gen. 2:16–17).

> **We don't try to solve our friends' problems or become all to them.**

While in the wilderness, Satan tempted Jesus to break through His human limitations and to jump from the highest point of the temple (Matt. 4:5–6).

Satan will continually tempt us to break through our limitations rather than accepting them as God's provision for our lives. When we embrace our limitations, we grow in humility and our friendships benefit. We don't try to solve our friends' problems or become all to them. We simply recognize that we are human and offer ourselves as a friend who trusts God to provide.

GROWING IN HUMILITY

Find an Opportunity to Serve

Rather than waiting for opportunities to come to you, look for opportunities to serve others. You don't need to wait to be asked if the single mom raising her kids would like to go out for an evening and how you could help that happen. What about that new person at work who's having a hard time adjusting to the workload? Who might need meds picked up at the pharmacy or their dog walked? When we look for opportunities to serve others, our humility grows. We recognize that we are called to partner with Jesus in serving others.

Learn to Ask for Help

Beyond serving others we also need to give others the opportunity to serve us. Many of us value independence but again, as I said earlier in this chapter, nowhere in Scripture is independence affirmed. We are to live connected to one another and sharing in sorrows, joys, needs, and burdens. In light of that, at times we must ask for help.

In the early church we learn that people didn't have outstanding needs because they took care of one another. They shared everything they had (Acts 4:32). When someone had a need they asked for help and others rallied around them. Imagine the early church and someone asking, "Hey, we're out of grain, does anyone have any?" Or, "Friends, my kids don't have warm clothes for this winter and we need blankets; anyone have extra?" Then the believers graciously and joyfully pooled their resources to help each other. They lived in community with each other. This is God's design for the church today. Like my friend Courtney, we must learn to ask for help when we need it. Not only will our burdens seem lighter, but we'll grow in humility.

Cultivate Curiosity

If you want to grow in humility, be intentional about cultivating curiosity. It takes practice. Shift your focus from your concerns to being curious about your friend's concerns. Ask questions. Seek to understand. Offer empathy. Don't give advice unless asked.

The ancient church father Ignatius wrote, "We will observe that the Fathers forbid us to give advice to our neighbor of our own accord, without our neighbor's asking us to do so. The voluntary giving of advice is a sign that we regard ourselves as possessed of spiritual knowledge and worth, which is a clear sign of pride and self-deception."[7]

Ouch! Right?! I wish I could say that I have never given anyone advice they didn't ask for. But I can't. I stand guilty, and so at night before I go to sleep, I confess that tendency as pride before the Lord and I ask that He would forgive me and help me remember to listen lovingly to others.

Practice Restraint

Not everything needs to be said. Proverbs 18:2 (esv) is such a great reminder for us: "A fool takes no pleasure in understanding, but only in expressing his opinion." In our day of social media obsession and political polarization, don't be quick to air your opinion. Instead, practice restraint as an act of humility. You won't agree with everything your friends say, but the beautiful thing is, you don't have to. Instead, focus on building bridges around the issues that you can agree on. Trust the Holy Spirit to bring correction or clarity on the issues around which you disagree. Focus your attention on listening and loving, and your friendships will grow much deeper. Be ready, relying on the Holy Spirit, to share with "everyone who asks you to give the reason for the hope" you have in Christ (1 Peter 3:15).

Invite Feedback

One of the most humble questions I have ever been asked is, "How do you experience me?" In other words, "How am I coming across?" I dare you to ask that question. It's a risk for sure. You don't have a guarantee of how the other person will respond. However, when you open yourself vulnerably with that question you are given deeper insight into whether or not others experience you as humble.

The psalmist asked such a profound question that I have returned to time and time again: "But who can discern their own errors?" (Ps. 19:12). Wow! It's hard to see and admit our own errors. Right?! We're often completely unaware. This is why we need a little help from our friends. True friends will help us discern our blind spots without shaming us for those faults. They keep us from becoming prideful and arrogant. Through their feedback we grow a little more in humility and gratefulness for God's continued grace.

PRAYER FOR HUMILITY

As we close this chapter, I am aware that I have given you much to think about. Author Andrew Murray, the old South African preacher, wrote, "The deepest humility is the secret of the truest happiness, of a joy that nothing can destroy."[8]

I realize the older I get that I must continually ask God for a heart of humility. It's so easy to forget, and pride creeps in the shadows lurking as insecurity, or self-preservation, or defensiveness. I have learned that even when I don't feel like it, I must ask God to mold my heart into the humility of Christ's heart. So friend, I offer you this prayer. Take it and make it your own.

Blessed Lord Jesus, I praise You for Your matchless example of humility. Though all of heaven was rightfully Yours, You left in obedience to the Father. My desires sometimes war within me, wanting to move forward and upward when You actually call me to step back and down in favor of others. Teach me, Holy Spirit, what it means to embrace humility. Show me what it looks like to offer others friendship out of a humble heart. Form in me the heart of a humble servant, I pray. Help me rest in You, knowing that in You, I am fully loved, forgiven, accepted, and desired.

DIGGING DEEPER INTO CONNECTION

Deeper Connection with God

1. Read the following verses and write a sentence next to each describing how the humility of Christ is seen.

   John 5:30
   John 8:28
   Luke 22:27
   Philippians 2:5–11

2. How might a deeper understanding of Christ's love help you to engage your friends with a humble heart?

3. How might experiencing God's presence more deeply help you embrace humility more effectively?

Deeper Connection with Yourself

1. In what areas of life have you felt insecure lately?

2. All of us need affirmation, but how might your need for approval get in the way of your desire to show up humble?

3. *When was the last time you honestly admitted that you were wrong, and asked for forgiveness?*

Deeper Connection with Others

1. *When you think of growing in humility, what are some of the habits the Lord is calling you to let go of?*

2. *Ask two people how you come across when someone confronts you. Often defensiveness is a sign that we need to grow in humility.*

3. *Try having a conversation with a friend and practice not giving any opinion, just remaining curious.*

God Demonstrated Humility through Jesus

"Come to me, all you who are weary and burdened, and I will give you rest. Take my yoke upon you and learn from me, for I am gentle and humble in heart, and you will find rest for your souls" (Matt. 11:28–30).

"You call me 'Teacher' and 'Lord' and rightly so, for that is what I am. Now that I, your Lord and Teacher, have washed your feet, you also should wash one another's feet. I have set you an example that you should do as I have done for you" (John 13:13–15).

"My grace is sufficient for you, for my power is made perfect in weakness" (2 Cor. 12:9).

"In your relationships with one another, have the same mindset as Christ Jesus: Who being in very nature God, did not consider equality with God something to be used to his own advantage; rather, he made himself nothing by taking the very nature of a servant, being made in human likeness. And being found in appearance as a man, he humbled himself by becoming obedient to death—even death on a cross!" (Phil. 2:5–8).

MARGARET'S STORY

Margaret is one of the kindest and most encouraging people you'll ever meet. I once asked her how she learned the skill of encouragement and she told me a story.

Years before, she found herself in a pattern of noting small faults in others. She told me she admitted this pattern to the Lord and asked forgiveness. One day while out shopping she spotted a glass hot air balloon. Margaret bought the object and set it on her windowsill where it could catch the light streaming in. It was a daily reminder to her that she wanted her words to be those that would bring light to others and encourage them.

When Margaret first moved to a new community, she and her husband found a new church that had a very different worship style from their former one, but Margaret refused to criticize. When I asked her how she adjusted to the change, she replied, "Oh, Becky, worship is not about me. It's about God." I love that! In an age of entitlement, when many are critical, Margaret's kind perspective is refreshing!

A few years ago, Margaret lost her husband of over fifty years. Dan was one of the most godly men I had ever known. When I called Margaret to see how she was coping, she told me about the people she was trying to encourage. While she misses Dan terribly, she takes initiative to reach out to others with kindness. She invites other widowed neighbors in for dinners, invites friends over for coffee and tea, and offers them all a listening ear. When Margaret notices others are feeling lonely, she reaches out with kindness and compassion, offering them friendship. As a result, Margaret's loneliness decreases.

CHAPTER THREE

Let Go of a Critical Spirit

Be kind and compassionate to one another.

EPHESIANS 4:32

As we embrace our humanness, we give
those around us permission to do the same.

HOLLEY GERTH

I remember how tense my stomach became during the course of a conversation I had years ago. Seated in a coffee shop across from an acquaintance, I heard many critical comments about her friends and family members. During the same conversation the dear woman confided in me that she was wrestling with terrible loneliness. She couldn't figure out how to find deep connections. At the end of our hour together, I felt exhausted from all the negativity, and I was ready to bolt.

Here's the thing. I can't judge my friend because sometimes I've had a critical attitude myself. Even if I haven't said it out loud, there have been times I've criticized someone silently for the way they've handled their marriage, or for the way they've raised their kids, or for their political views, or for the post they shared on social media. In recent years, I've become more aware of this tendency in myself and have asked the Holy Spirit to be ruthless with me in uprooting these thoughts, because the truth is, it's wrong to judge others.

Often the reason for our loneliness is because we've become known for being critical. To put it simply, people are not longing to be with someone who has a judgmental spirit. They are drawn to those who are kind and gracious. Often the loneliest people are those who wrestle the most with a fault-finding attitude.

We are living in a time in history where judgmentalism, criticism, and polarization have grown to epic proportions. In our present culture, we can no longer disagree with each other. If we disagree with someone's opinion or lifestyle, our culture now accuses us of being a hater or some kind of "phobe." No wonder we have become polarized! The truth is that love doesn't mean we always agree. Love means we are kind to each other even when we disagree.

Jesus warned us in no uncertain terms that we are not to cultivate a critical attitude (John 7:24). His words cut through any false pretense we might have that we are helping others by correcting them. A critical attitude not only erodes our relationships, but it boomerangs back on us. What results is a cycle of fault-finding. One thing is for sure: the more you criticize others, the lonelier you are going to feel. What if, instead of focusing on another's faults, we focused on finding the beauty in each other? Imagine what rich relationships we would enjoy.

Paul wanted the believers in Ephesus to enjoy deep connections and community. He wrote and reminded them to "be kind and compassionate to one another" (Eph. 4:32). The idea behind the word *kind* that is used by Paul is "serviceable, good, pleasant and gracious."[1] So simple. So profound. Paul used the same word when he wrote to the church in Galatia. He told them that one evidence a person is filled with the Holy Spirit is kindness (Gal. 5:22).

Kindness and compassion are very similar. Yet there is a slight difference. Compassion speaks to having a soft heart toward others—it is a feeling. A tenderhearted person is warm and caring. They're willing to consider views other than their own. They are slow to criticize others and quick to overlook faults. Kindness speaks to taking action on those feelings. Paul invites us to feel compassion for others but then to act on those feelings, demonstrating kindness in tangible ways.

The question then is, how do we bring both compassion and kindness into our relationships? One tangible way to excel in both is to let go of our tendency to criticize. In our current cancel culture, we've become so comfortable with criticizing others that at times I don't even think we're aware we're doing it. In light of that, before we go any further, let's pause and consider. Let's examine ourselves honestly to see if we have a tendency to criticize others.

"DO I HAVE A CRITICAL ATTITUDE?"

To help raise our awareness, here are just a few signs that you might be wrestling with a critical attitude. Remember, it is our own sinful nature that trips us up even when we don't want to do what is wrong in God's eyes and harmful to others. Even Paul wrestled with his sinful nature, and you can read about his famous frustration with himself in Romans 7:14–21. The fact that he—and we—care about conquering our sinful tendencies shows that we do belong to the Lord and love Him. But we absolutely can't leave it there as though our sin, including a tendency toward a critical attitude or spirit, doesn't matter. I want you to realize how serious this is. So here are a few warning signs that indicate you are wrestling with a critical spirit:

- You find yourself internally judging others for how they raise their kids.
- You give unwarranted advice without being invited because you feel the need to correct.
- You tell others what they did wrong and try to give them helpful tips to improve.
- You accuse others of having faulty motives.
- You find fault with the skill set of others.
- You are easily frustrated when others don't meet your expectations.

When we criticize and judge others, we are pointing the finger at them. We might not say things out loud, but internally we're shaking our heads and scolding them in our minds. I asked a few friends what they most often felt judged about. Here are some of the answers I received:

- eating habits
- upkeep and appearance of homes and cars
- spiritual practices
- spending habits
- political views
- lifestyle in general, including child-rearing

Wow! Is it any wonder that we're wrestling with loneliness?

Let me give you an example from my own life. I remember when I had four young children. I tried really hard to keep my house clean but often activities, toddlers, and babies got in the way of my best intentions. I'll never forget inviting a potential friend over to coffee. Before long she proceeded to tell me how I could keep my stairs cleaner by using a sponge. I was polite and thanked her. But are you surprised that I never invited her over again? I was looking for friendship, not cleaning advice!

JUDGMENT AND DISCERNMENT: WHAT'S THE DIFFERENCE?

Now before we go any further, I know what you're thinking: "Becky, what about discernment? Are you saying we shouldn't judge between right and wrong?" No. Scripture calls us to be discerning as far as the ways of holiness.

For example, the apostle John tells us that we are to "test the spirits to see whether they are from God" (1 John 4:1). This means we are to discern whether a theological point of view squares with Scripture. If it doesn't, we don't embrace it. Scripture is always the final authority on discerning between what's right and wrong.

Discernment is about making wise decisions. It's not about criticizing or accusing another person. I love the way the book of Proverbs describes the person of discernment: "The wise in heart are called discerning: and gracious words promote instruction" (Prov. 16:21). Solomon goes on to describe gracious words, "Gracious words are a honeycomb, sweet to the soul and healing to the bones" (Prov. 16:21, 24). Pause for just a moment and consider.

When you are criticizing another person, are your words sweet to that person's soul? Are they life-giving? I'm guessing not.

Here's the bottom line. We are not to focus on finding fault with others. Jesus questioned, "Why do you look at the speck of sawdust in your brother's eye and pay no attention to the plank in your own eye? How can you say to your brother, 'Let me take the speck out of your eye,' when all the time there is a plank in your own eye? You hypocrite, first take the plank out of your own eye, and then you will see clearly to remove the speck from your brother's eye" (Matt. 7:3–5).

> **Each of us has enough problems in our own lives. Instead of finding fault, we are to serve and love one another.**

To be just a bit facetious, we could paraphrase this as "Why do you look at the speck of dust on someone else's stairs before removing the dust balls on your own stairs? Or why do you judge the Cheerios on the floor of your friend's car without considering the cookie crumbs in your own car? Or why do you judge the behavior of a toddler throwing a fit in Target when your own teen is pulling away from you and angry all the time?"

The point is that each of us has enough problems in our own personal lives. We don't have the right to judge someone else's life. Often, we don't have all the information about what's going on in another person's life anyway. Instead of finding fault, we are to serve and love one another.

I saw this post on Instagram and I absolutely love it! "It's hard to throw stones if you're busy washing someone's feet!"[2] Don't you just love that?! In other words, if your focus is on serving and lifting others up, it's going to be awfully hard to judge them.

I remember many years ago when a friend I loved made a choice I strongly disagreed with. I was on my knees in prayer early one morning, when I felt the Holy Spirit speak to me. "Becky, if you are without sin, here's a rock, you can throw it!" Ouch!

John told a story in his gospel about Jesus. While the story is not included in the earliest manuscripts, most Bible commentators agree that the story actually happened. If you have your Bible handy, turn to John 8.

In this engaging account, Jesus was teaching in the temple courts when the Pharisees burst in dragging a woman caught in adultery. Quoting the law of Moses, the Pharisees reminded Jesus that the law stated she should be stoned. This poor woman! The Pharisees didn't mention the man she was with, they only accused her. Hardly concerned about holiness, they were trying to trap Jesus. Jesus bent down and starting writing with His finger on the ground. Wouldn't you love to know what He was writing? Then He said, "Let any one of you who is without sin be the first to throw a stone at her" (John 8:7). One by one her accusers left. I always found it interesting that the older ones left first—age and experience should bring some wisdom! Jesus straightened up and asked the woman where everyone had gone. "Has no one condemned you?" She replied, "No one, sir." And Jesus said, "Then neither do I condemn you. Go now and leave your life of sin" (John 8:10–12).

The question for you and me to consider is, if Jesus didn't condemn the woman, but instead offered compassion and kindness, shouldn't we follow His lead? Sit with that question for a few minutes. When we criticize others, we are condemning them instead of offering grace, and the truth is each of us needs grace in our relationships. Think about it:

We forget appointments. We run late to meet friends. We sometimes miss deadlines. We might not be at our best at all times. We get cranky and say rude things. On occasion we're awkward. In short, we need compassion and kindness rather than criticism. So next time your spouse or friend completely messes up, what would it look like for you to echo the words of Jesus and say, "Don't worry. I don't condemn you!"

As we live day to day in our increasingly polarized culture, how do we bring kindness back into our relationships? How do we offer compassion and understanding in our friendships?

BRING BACK KINDNESS

As we think about bringing kindness back into our relationships, here are a few practical steps to get you started.

Offer Compassionate Understanding

Author and speaker Kirk Walden, while speaking at a pro-life banquet for Hope Center Ministries in Greenville, North Carolina, said, "When people surround you with compassion it changes everything."[3] Walden was making the case that compassionate understanding will change our culture. I wholeheartedly agree. Too often, rather than offering compassion, we criticize.

The psalmist wisely prayed, "Set a guard over my mouth, LORD" (Ps. 141:3). In today's culture we might expand that prayer to "Set a guard not only over my mouth, Lord, but also over my posts on social media. Don't let me criticize or destroy others with anything I post on social media." Like Walden was pointing out, culture is not going to change because you point out how wrong people are. Use social media to offer encouragement rather than rebukes.

For example, people often share news and requests for prayer on social media, which can take some courage, as we can see sometimes in the comments below a post. "Please pray for me because I'm having surgery and I'm nervous about it," someone may request. Perhaps a hundred people will respond with a message of kindness and hope—but there's that one who says, "I don't trust doctors. Didn't you try a natural remedy? There must be sin in your life." Unfortunately, it's often the negative comments that stick with us.

The wise writer of Proverbs wrote, "The tongue has the power of life and death" (Prov. 18:21). Don't destroy others with your words. Instead, be the person who is known for never saying an unkind word about anyone.

In your relationships, seek to understand, rather than correcting or rebuking. I've never seen someone change their belief system or their behavior because they were scolded. Have you? If you become known for being a person who scolds others, or corrects often, it's likely you will lose friends. Instead, seek to understand others. When they feel heard and valued, they'll want to hang with you more.

Discover the Joy of Empathy

Empathy tells another person, "Your thoughts and feelings make sense to me." Some have described it as the ability to walk in another's shoes. When Paul wrote, "Rejoice with those who rejoice; mourn with those who mourn" (Rom. 12:15), he was describing empathy.

Empathy makes us feel deeply connected to others, and it is an essential quality if we are to let go of loneliness. Science confirms this. In *How to Listen So People Will Talk*, I quoted research that has uncovered "mirror neurons."[4] "The neurons are located in our brain and wired to respond to the emotions of others so that we can mirror their feelings."[5]

Here's how this works. Suppose you're out to lunch with a friend who is struggling with a coworker. Tensions are high around the office and arguments are erupting. As a result, your friend is discouraged. Rather than telling them how to fix the problem, lean in (literally), let your friend see compassion in your eyes, and offer kindness by affirming, "Wow, that would be frustrating to me as well." Then, you might ask, "How can I pray with you as you move forward in this situation?" When your friend feels understood, you'll both feel more connected!

Or, maybe when you're with a friend having coffee, she shares that her finances have been hard and discouraging. Rather than suggesting to her that she get a handle on her debt and take a class, acknowledge that financial pressures feel awful and produce anxiety. Seek to let her know that her feelings make sense to you. A little empathy goes a long way in cultivating deeper connections.

Practical Acts of Kindness

Practical acts of kindness that flow from a compassionate heart are the best. Suppose for a minute that you have a friend whose little ones are all sick with the stomach flu. You feel compassion for her. I mean, the stomach flu is the worst, right?! Beyond just feeling bad for your friend, take initiative and deliver some clear soup and crackers to her front door.

With a little thought and effort on your part you can be an extension of the kindness of God in someone's life. Amber knew that Samantha was in the middle of an absolutely crazy season. Between work, finishing her degree, and raising three kids, Samantha was behind on housework. Amber decided to surprise her friend by hiring a cleaning service, and while they were at Samantha's house, Amber washed, dried, and folded the children's laundry. What a practical way to offer kindness! We all need friends who will go out of their way to help us every now and then. Why not be that friend to someone else? I guarantee your friend will want a deeper connection with you.

Resign as the Truth Police

Another tangible way to bring kindness back is to let go of the need to be the "truth police." What do I mean? In case you're unfamiliar, the truth police is the person who will correct you mid-story because you might have remembered one detail incorrectly. Here's the thing—no one wants to be corrected mid-story. In fact, psychologists will tell you that being the truth police can damage the connection and intimacy between people. Instead, remind yourself that it's okay if your friend or spouse gets some details of what happened wrong. It likely won't matter in twenty years anyway. Let it go.

Don't Assume You Know Someone's Motives

Another good rule of thumb is don't imagine you know the motives of another. Maybe your friend has seemingly "ghosted" you, that is, suddenly stopped communicating. You're offended and hurt and ready to ditch the relationship. You assume she's angry or has moved on to more advantageous friendships. Don't make assumptions about what's going on in her head. Instead, reach out, ask a few good questions, and try to figure out what's going on in her life. Likely, what feels like ghosting really has nothing to do with you. Change your narrative! Instead of thinking, "She's probably mad" or "She's so busy she doesn't have time for me," think instead, "I wonder what difficulties or stresses she is facing that has made it challenging to connect." Then maybe send a card or handwritten note to that friend affirming positive qualities you see in her life.

Here's another scenario. You've looked forward to lunch together, but your colleague has canceled three times in a row. Rather than jumping to conclusions about why, change the story in your head. Recognize that you don't know their motive. It might have nothing to do with you. Instead of throwing stones in your mind, seek to understand and offer grace. Here's what I know: the more grace you give, the more friends you will enjoy.

Most of us who call ourselves believers are trying our best to pursue Jesus and keep our families intact. We mess up. We get it wrong sometimes. We fail sometimes. What we need in those moments is compassion and grace, not judgment or criticism. After all, it's the kindness of God that leads us to repentance (Rom. 2:4). God's kindness goes exceedingly beyond all we can imagine. Though He is absolute perfection, He continues to offer compassion instead of condemnation. How can we who are not perfect ourselves offer anything less?

HOW THE BIBLE DESCRIBES KINDNESS

As we close this chapter, I think it would be good for us to do an exercise with Paul's famous love chapter. You see, dear friend, Paul's words are the perfect description of God's kindness. If we want to follow His lead, we need to ask the Holy Spirit to develop these characteristics in our lives. In order to better understand the gravity of this, I suggest reading the following words from 1 Corinthians 13:4–7 out loud but substitute the word "love" with your own name. It will give you a true picture of how closely you are living in sync with God's compassion. Here's what that looks like with my name.

Becky is patient,
Becky is kind.
She does not envy,
she does not boast,
she is not proud.
She does not dishonor (or criticize) others,
she is not self-seeking,
she is not easily angered,
she keeps no record of wrongs.
Becky does not delight in evil
but she rejoices with the truth.
She always protects,
always trusts, always hopes,
always perseveres.

When I read it out loud like this, I am deeply convicted and reminded that it is not my place to be judgmental or critical. Satan is the accuser. I am not to be anything like him. I am to follow the way of Christ, which is compassion. How about you? Is it convicting for you? If so, let's agree to give others grace and compassion. Imagine how different the body of Christ would look if we all chose that posture.

Take a moment and pray this prayer with me.

Lord Jesus, make me an instrument of Your compassion and kindness today. May others feel grace radiating from my life. Curb in me any tendency to criticize. Where there are critical thoughts, replace them with compassionate ones. Show me how to tangibly demonstrate kindness in my family, friendships, and community. Let me be known more for how I love others than for what I am against.

DIGGING DEEPER INTO CONNECTION

Deeper Connection with God

1. Look up the following verses and consider what they teach you about kindness and compassion.

   Psalm 103:1–8
   Galatians 5:22
   Colossians 3:12

2. Read Matthew 9:36–37. In what ways did Jesus illustrate both compassion and kindness in this story? List all the ways you can think of and then reflect on what this story teaches you. What do you feel like God is saying to you?

Deeper Connection with Yourself

1. How have you experienced the kindness of God in your life?

2. What most often prevents you from doing acts of kindness for others?

3. *When have you felt compassion for someone and acted on those feelings?*

4. *How have critical words hurt you in the past? Spend some time releasing those words to the Lord and ask Him to heal the wounds they created.*

Deeper Connection with Others

1. *Who do you know that exemplifies kindness and compassion in everyday life?*

2. *When was the last time you experienced kindness from a friend? Take a few moments and write them a thank-you note and put it in the mail.*

3. *What is one act of kindness you could do this week for one of your friends? (Think practically.)*

God Demonstrates Kindness and Compassion

"As a father has compassion on his children, so the LORD has compassion on those who fear him; for he knows how we are formed, he remembers that we are dust" (Ps. 103:13–14).

"'Though the mountains be shaken and the hills be removed, yet my unfailing love for you will not be shaken nor my covenant of

peace be removed,' says the LORD, *who has compassion on you"*
(Isa. 54:10).

"In order that in the coming ages he might show the
incomparable riches of his grace, expressed in his kindness to us
in Christ Jesus" (Eph. 2:7).

"But when the kindness and love of God our Savior appeared,
he saved us, not because of righteous things we had done, but
because of his mercy. He saved us through the washing of rebirth
and renewal by the Holy Spirit" (Titus 3:4–5).

JILL'S STORY

I met Jill during a rough season in my life. The church my husband pastored was filled with division and conflict. While Steve was trying to navigate his role and all the conflicts among staff, I was trying to navigate recovering from cancer and fears that new cancer had invaded my body.

Jill and I became friends and began getting together to converse about the things the Lord was teaching us. Though Jill and her husband, Greg, wrestled with infertility, they were never bitter, but instead kept reaching out to others. They invested heavily in the emotional and spiritual life of my children. Often at the dinner table we'd have spiritual conversations and then play games with the kids. At times, they'd just stop in and help with homework and share snacks. I used to joke with Jill that "four kids are a lot, which is why we need four parents in the mix!"

After a few years Steve and I felt God's leading to move to Colorado. I dreaded leaving Jill. She had become like a sister to me.

A few days before our departure, I shared my fears with Jill. How would our friendship survive long-distance? Jill paused and then shared that she deeply valued loyalty. She promised not only to be faithful in our friendship, but also to faithfully be a surrogate aunt to our kids.

It's now twenty years later, and Jill and I are as close as ever. She remembers all my kids' birthdays, as well as their spouses' and their kids' birthdays. And for the record, that's fourteen grandchildren! We talk by phone regularly and pray for each other faithfully. Through the years, Jill has taught me much about the beauty of loyalty in friendship.

CHAPTER FOUR

Develop Loyalty

Be devoted to one another.

ROMANS 12:10

These days we trade churches and jobs and neighborhoods and cars without batting an eyelash. But there is power in the staying. Loyalty is perhaps one of the greatest virtues next to love and faith. It's not just for the dogs, it's for the people too.

JENNIFER LEE DUKES

I remember several years ago meeting up for lunch with a friend. As we sat sipping our delicious soup, my friend was sharing with me about a rejection she had faced recently. Someone she had been a close friend with for several years was suddenly unavailable; she no longer had time to get together or even talk by phone. Apparently the effort to continue the friendship was too difficult, and now this once close friend had moved on to a new group of companions. As I listened, I thought, *How sad!* From my perspective, life is too short to not have loyal friends.

Loyalty seems to be a forgotten value in our culture. Spouses leave marriages in search of someone better, congregants leave churches because they've been offended, friends ditch friendships because life has become too busy, volunteers drop off when the activity is no longer fun. In the absence of loyalty, we can be plunged into the abyss of loneliness. Only through the commitment of faithful, loving loyalty can we enjoy the community God designed us to experience.

A BEAUTIFUL EXAMPLE OF LOYALTY

Here's how I would define loyalty:

> Loyalty is faithfully, steadfastly,
> and devotedly loving another person.

Loyalty sticks with the relationship (barring abuse) and accepts others for who they are. It does not leave when there is conflict. It provides a deep sense of belonging in our disconnected world. We are called to this type of steadfast commitment in our relationships with one another.

One of my favorite stories is about two women, Ruth and Naomi. A daughter-in-law and her mother-in-law. An unlikely pair for deep friendship. One was a Moabite and one was Jewish. That in and of itself was a problem. But let's start at the beginning.

There was a famine in the land, which affected the town of Bethlehem. Scripture tells us about a couple, Elimelek and Naomi, who together with their two sons left Bethlehem and moved down to Moab. While there, the two sons married Moabite women, Orpah and Ruth.

After some time, Naomi's husband died, and her two sons died as well. That's a lot of loss! Naomi was grieving and distraught. I can't imagine the depth of her pain! She heard that the famine was over and that God had provided for His people in Bethlehem, so she set out to return to her hometown. Let's pause there for just a moment.

Isn't it ironic—Elimelek left the land of God's provision for something better? How often in our lives do you and I when we encounter difficulty, whether in a relationship or in our careers, bail out and head for greener pastures? Rather than trusting God to provide, we leave the place of God's provision and blessing in a knee-jerk reaction to trials. Friend, that never turns out well.

Naomi heard that God had

> *Ruth chose to stay with her mother-in-law. What would inspire her to have such loyalty for Naomi? It couldn't have been easy.*

provided in Bethlehem and decided to return. Her daughters-in-law began to make the trek with her; however, Naomi encouraged them to go back to their homeland of Moab and to their own families instead. Orpah kissed her mother-in-law on the cheek and, with much weeping, headed back to Moab. Ruth, however, replied with these beautiful words: "Don't urge me to leave you or to turn back from you. Where you go I will go, and where you stay I will stay. Your people will be my people and your God my God" (Ruth 1:16). Ah, what a beautiful declaration of loyalty!

Ruth must have known that it would be a long, treacherous journey back to Bethlehem. She likely understood that as a Moabite woman the chances were high that, once there, she would not be treated well by the locals. Yet, Ruth chose to stay with her mother-in-law.

What would inspire Ruth to have such loyalty for Naomi? She obviously loved her mother-in-law. However, I believe there was something deeper pulling her. At the center of her decision was a cavernous ache to know the God she had seen evidence of in Naomi's life. God Himself lured Ruth into pledging her allegiance to Naomi knowing that she would ultimately find the belonging her soul longed for in Him. It's as if I can hear God Himself whispering in Ruth's ear what He would speak through a prophet hundreds of years later: "I have loved you with an everlasting love; I have drawn you with unfailing kindness" (Jer. 31:3).

Let's return to the story.

When they arrived in Bethlehem, Ruth recognized that Naomi was wiped out and still grieving. Yet, they needed to eat, so Ruth offered to find a way to earn a living. She would do the menial task of picking up grain left in the fields by harvesters. God had commanded His people, "When you reap the harvest of your land, do not reap to the very edges of your field or gather the gleanings of your harvest. Leave them for the poor and for the foreigner residing among you" (Lev. 23:22). I love the tenderness of God Almighty to take care of the poor and the refugee. Ruth must have learned about this law, and so she went to the field to work and find food.

Interestingly, the name "Ruth" has its roots in the Hebrew meaning "companion or friend."[1] Those who are loyal friends experience far less loneliness than those who run at the first sign of difficulty. It couldn't have been easy for Ruth to stay with Naomi, especially when Naomi was morose due to all the grieving. Yet, Ruth stood by Naomi's side faithfully. She was loyal and faithful to her mother-in-law and ultimately was able to bless Naomi with a grandson who would be in the lineage of Jesus, our ultimate model of loyalty.

GOD'S VERY NATURE IS LOYAL

Even when the disciples, Jesus' closest friends, abandoned and denied Him, Jesus remained faithful and loyal. Remember when Peter disowned Jesus in the courtyard? Three times to be exact! He claimed he didn't even know Jesus. Yet, Jesus remained loyal. Later, after the resurrection, Jesus made Peter breakfast on the beach. He asked him three times, "Do you love me?" (John 21:15–17).

Friend, the truth is it is God's very nature to remain loyal to us. I cherish the words of Paul who wrote, "I am convinced that neither death nor life, neither angels nor demons, neither the present nor the future, nor any powers, neither height nor depth, nor anything else in all creation, will be able to separate us from the love of God that is in Christ Jesus our Lord" (Rom. 8:38–39). Jesus is the ultimate loyal friend! For Him to abandon or give up on us would essentially be impossible, as it would contradict His very nature. Those who are believers are now "in Christ" (2 Cor. 5:17).

We are Christ's body (1 Cor. 12:27) and if He were to be disloyal to us, He would be disloyal to Himself. Paul wrote to Timothy, "if we are faithless, he remains faithful, for he cannot disown himself" (2 Tim. 2:13). Did you catch that? God can't be disloyal because He can't disown Himself! Wow! Is that reassuring or what?

Now, I know what you're thinking. Isn't there a time when we should not prioritize loyalty? Yes. Let's look at some common misconceptions about loyalty to clarify.

COMMON MISCONCEPTIONS ABOUT LOYALTY

Being Loyal Is Not Being Blind to Faults

Every human person is going to have faults, your friends included. Therefore, every one of your relationships will have pitfalls. Loyalty doesn't mean you deny faults. Loyalty means you love in spite of faults. Like Solomon wrote, "love covers over all wrongs" (Prov. 10:12). This doesn't mean you exonerate all wrongs and ignore them. You might need to speak the truth in love, but you remain in the friendship unless it becomes toxic . . . which leads me to the next misconception.

Being Loyal Doesn't Mean You Stay in a Toxic or Unhealthy Friendship

Every now and then, friendships become unhealthy and even toxic. When a friendship becomes unhealthy, creating anxiety within you or filling you with self-doubt or becoming too possessive, it's time to put some space in the relationship. Loyalty doesn't imply that you stay in a friendship that is continually hurting you or trying to control you. How can you tell if a friendship is toxic or unhealthy? Here are a few signs:

WARNING SIGNS OF A TOXIC FRIENDSHIP:

- A friend disrespects your boundaries.
- A friend becomes overly possessive/jealous when you hang out with other friends.
- A friend doesn't take responsibility when they hurt you. They never genuinely apologize.

◆ A friend becomes overly needy and dependent on you. They drain and exhaust you, always taking and never giving.

When you start seeing these signs, you need to back up a bit and do some reflecting on your own personal boundaries. Boundaries make good neighbors and, similarly, respecting the boundaries of others builds strong friendships. Our boundaries define what's ours to possess or control, and what's not ours to possess or control.

Boundaries were God's idea. In fact, He gave His people this law in the Old Testament: "Do not move your neighbor's boundary stone set up by your predecessors [ancestors] in the inheritance you receive in the land the LORD your God is giving you to possess" (Deut. 19:14). We could paraphrase this verse as a rule for our lives, saying, "You are not to violate your friends' boundaries or try to manipulate them into changing their boundaries."

Some friends might go through an unhealthy season, and it's fine to be there for them as long as you can keep your own boundaries in place. However, if you are continually being hurt, that's a different story and leads us to the next misconception.

Being Loyal Doesn't Mean You Put Up with Abuse

When a relationship becomes abusive, you need to get out quickly and seek help. If you are being emotionally or physically bullied at home or at work, name it and tell someone. Ignoring or allowing abuse has nothing to do with trying to remain loyal. Leave the situation and get some godly counseling to help you decide on next steps. Find a Christian therapist in your area who can help you escape the abuser. If necessary, you might have to take legal measures. It is not God's will for you to be abused.*

Now that we've clarified some misconceptions, let's take a look at what loyalty looks like in a healthy friendship.

WHAT DOES LOYALTY LOOK LIKE
IN A HEALTHY FRIENDSHIP?

Remaining Trustworthy

Who are the friends you've had for more than five years, ten years, or even twenty years? Have you kept their confidences, or have you ever shared secrets that were not yours to share? Take a moment to pause and think. If you have broken confidences, then confess that to the Lord, ask His forgiveness, and move forward, asking the Holy Spirit to build trustworthiness in you.

The wise writer of Proverbs wrote, "Do not betray another's confidence" (Prov. 25:9). At the very core of loyalty is the ability to keep the confidences of another. Your faithfulness in keeping confidences over time whispers that the relationship is important to you, and you can be trusted to remain loyal.

Protecting Another's Reputation

I fear this is a lost art in today's culture. We are so quick to judge and criticize. Loyalty, however, defends the reputation of others. I love the way David writes, "Who may live on your holy mountain? The one whose walk is blameless, who does what is

---

* Sometimes women come to believe being abused is their fault or even that somehow they are "suffering for Christ." Hear me: it is not God's will for you to be abused. If you are in this situation, tell someone who can help you: a pastor, a Christian counselor, even the law.

righteous, who speaks the truth from their heart; whose tongue utters no slander, who does no wrong to a neighbor, and casts no slur on others" (Ps. 15:1–3).

Did you catch that last bit of instruction to not slander others? In other words, be someone who doesn't raise even a hint of concern about another's reputation. We can cast a slur on another by simply raising doubts about their integrity, or even sharing something couched as a prayer request. On the flip side, when you are loyal to someone, you refuse to tarnish their reputation in any way. Instead, you speak positively about them, even when they're not present.

Celebrating the Wins of Your Friend

When you are loyal to your friend you will celebrate their victories. You won't get caught up in the trap of comparison; instead, you'll focus on them and celebrate their wins.

Remember Jill, whom I wrote about in the beginning of this chapter? After my first book released, Jill sent me flowers in a beautiful pitcher that I still have to this day. What was she doing? She was celebrating with me the win of releasing my first book. I never forgot how great that felt and I have attempted to follow her lead in that area. When my friend Judy released her first book, I celebrated with her, bought her flowers, went to her book launch party, and have encouraged other people to buy the book. Why? Because that's what loyal friends do for each other. We celebrate the victories of our friends.

Sometimes, it's not the victories of accomplishments but the victories of answered prayer. I prayed with a friend about her marriage for over a year, and then there was a major breakthrough. Boy, did we celebrate the answer to prayer together!

Think back over this past year. Who of your friends have had a new baby, received a promotion at work, begun a new job, or received an honor of some sort for volunteer work they've done? Which of your friends have experienced great answers to prayer? Who has achieved a goal, such as memorizing a portion of Scripture, or taking off those ten pounds? How can you as a friend celebrate with them? If you want to feel less lonely, you'll put some effort into applauding the victories of others.

Prioritizing Time for Friends

All of us are busy. In some ways, busyness is the curse of our age. Many of us work long hours or are involved in a million different activities. However, if you truly want to treasure your friends and demonstrate your loyalty, you will create the space to spend time together. Job wrote, "anyone who withholds kindness from a friend forsakes the fear of the Almighty" (Job 6:14). I am convinced that one way we withhold kindness from friends is allowing our schedules to become so full that we simply don't have time for them. Years ago, it wasn't that way between friends.

> **They connected in person because friendships were the fabric of life.**

I remember my grandmother, Clara. Every summer I would spend a week with her in Brooklyn, New York. I went to her church's vacation Bible school and had a great time. My grandmother was Swedish. Every afternoon at around 3:00 she had Aunt Isabelle over for coffee and coffee cake. Aunt Isabelle wasn't really my aunt, she was just a close friend of my grandmother. But for years, afternoon coffee and coffee cake together was the pattern. My grandmother wasn't the only one. Getting together for afternoon tea or coffee was the norm for many in those days and in that place. Friends prioritized time together. It's probably true that life was a bit simpler then. There were no cellphones, internet, or social media. You just got together with your neighbors and church friends and you had coffee and pastries. You connected in person because friendships were the fabric of life.

My friend Jill told me that when she was growing up, the parents on her block used to take turns hosting their neighbors for appetizers after work. Whoever was hosting would simply raise the flag on their mailbox, and then whichever neighbors were available would stop in for a few appetizers and drinks. Imagine how well those neighbors knew each other!

My, how things have changed. Now, though we have things that are supposed to make our lives easier, we are busier than ever, and we're also lonelier than ever. Perhaps we need to reexamine our priorities. If we are loyal to our friends, we'll create the space to be with them.

IT'S TIME TO BRING BACK THE VIRTUE OF LOYALTY

Though we live in different times with all the opportunities that technology brings us, I believe it's time to return to the virtue of loyalty. In your world, let loyalty begin with you. Be intentional about being faithful in your relationships. Don't ditch your old friends in favor of new friends. Instead, cultivate each relationship with the attitude that the relationship is precious and worth investing in. I know for sure, dear reader, that this is part of your calling because you are invited to be transformed into the image of Christ. He Himself is the most loyal of all. Why don't you pause for just a moment and ask the Holy Spirit to develop this virtue in your life? As you cooperate with Him in your transformation, I believe you are going to experience far less loneliness because loyalty is a quality that others are drawn to.

Lord Jesus, I praise You that You are a loyal friend like no other. You demonstrated Your loyalty to me by loving me even when I was a sinner and by going to the cross to die for me. Thank You that You will never leave me nor forsake me. You are closer than any other. Help me today, to remember how loyal You are to me and then to demonstrate that commitment to my friends.

DIGGING DEEPER INTO CONNECTION

Deeper Connection with God

1. Read 2 Chronicles 16:9. How does this verse demonstrate that God values our loyalty to Him?

2. Read Hebrews 13:5. What does this verse teach you about God's loyalty?

3. In what ways have you personally experienced the loyalty of God in your life?

4. Not only is God loyal to us, but He asks us to be loyal to Him. What does loyalty to God look like, practically speaking, in your life?

Deeper Connection with Yourself

1. On a scale of 1–10, 1 being the least loyal and 10 being extremely loyal, how would you rate yourself as a friend in terms of loyalty?

2. *What most often gets in the way of you being a loyal friend?*

3. *Name the friendships that you have cultivated for over ten years. Then spend time praying for each of those friends.*

4. *Has there been a time when one of your friends broke your confidence? How did that impact your ability to offer trustworthy, loyal friendship to others?*

Deeper Connection with Others

1. *Choose two friends with whom you've been in friendship for over ten years. Write a note to each of them affirming qualities you love about them.*

2. *Host a party for a friend celebrating one of their accomplishments.*

3. *Fast from social media for a week and instead, schedule in-person time with several of your friends. For those who live at a distance, set up a time to chat by phone or Zoom. For those in the area, invite them over for coffee or tea and snacks.*

God Is Loyal

"Know therefore that the LORD *your God is God; he is the faithful God, keeping his covenant of love to a thousand generations"* (Deut. 7:9).

"Who shall separate us from the love of Christ? Shall trouble or hardship or persecution or famine or nakedness or danger or sword? . . . No, in all these things we are more than conquerors through him who loved us. For I am convinced that neither death nor life, neither angels nor demons, neither the present nor the future, nor any powers, neither height nor depth, nor anything else in all creation, will be able to separate us from the love of God in Christ Jesus our Lord" (Rom. 8:35, 37–39).

"If we are faithless, he remains faithful, for he cannot disown himself" (2 Tim. 2:13).

"Never will I leave you; never will I forsake you" (Heb. 13:5b).

"If we confess our sins, he is faithful and just and will forgive us our sins and purify us from all unrighteousness" (1 John 1:9).

MARLA'S STORY

Marla never set out to be alone. She was friendly with her coworkers and with people at church, but didn't really click with anyone or get involved after work or with church activities. And one after another, people she knew were pairing off. Church especially felt like a world of happy couples. She longed for the intimacy of marriage and envied what she saw in other people's marriages.

Not only were others happy in relationships, but they were surrounded by others socially. Other women met for coffee or joined committees. Other women lived in houses; Marla had an apartment. Other women cooked for their family. She zapped lasagna for one. Other women had careers. Marla had a job. As her loneliness increased, Marla felt she didn't matter anymore. That's when she realized things had to change, and that she had to make them change.

Rather than assume she knew about her coworkers and envy how they seemed superior to her, she decided to get to know them. She began to take initiative, inviting others to sit down for coffee or lunch. She soon learned that no one's life is perfect.

She also got involved at church. It took a while, but she slowly learned to open up to others about her own hopes and dreams. And in turn, as others opened up to her, she discovered that not everyone was part of a happy couple or lived problem-free.

Marla has a firm belief in God. She asks Him to strengthen her to live an intentional and productive life. As she leans into the security she has in Him and lets go of comparing, He eases her loneliness.

CHAPTER FIVE

Start Cheering, Stop Comparing

Let us not become conceited,
provoking one another,
envying one another.

GALATIANS 5:26 ESV

We fall apart when we look at our fears and inadequacies and
compare ourselves to every other runner. But fix your eyes on
a God like Jesus, and you will not quit.

JENNIE ALLEN

I sat across the table from my eleven-year-old granddaughter while we were eating lunch, and I asked, "Hey, Selah, what is God teaching you these days?" I happen to know that Selah has a deep relationship with God, so I felt comfortable asking her.

She paused for a few minutes and then she said, "Contentment!" Her answer shocked me. I mean how many sixth-grade girls do you know who are content? Selah went on to tell me that God was teaching her to be content with who she was and the sport she was doing. She had learned that in order to be content and enjoy great relationships she needed to start cheering for her friends and stop comparing!

Originally, I wondered whether or not I needed to write this chapter. I questioned, "Do people struggle with envy that much that it would interrupt their relationships?" Then the Holy Spirit spoke to my heart. As He examined my soul, I realized that comparing myself with others has been a lifelong battle for me, and at times envy has affected my relationships.

Sometimes we need a wake-up call from the Holy Spirit, right? There have been times when I've compared my body to the body of another and become discouraged. Even more so, I struggle with comparing achievements and accomplishments. This is a huge temptation for most of us who are in the business of being authors and speakers. Let me be completely honest, and please don't judge me. Just recently, I was browsing in a bookstore looking for a relaxing read when I stopped short. An acquaintance, younger than me and on her first book, hit the bestseller list. Immediately I felt discouragement hit my stomach! I know the author. I've had interactions with her. She's just getting started and has already hit the top. I compared my efforts and the books I've written and came up short.

In my heart, thoughts rose up, like, *She doesn't deserve to be on that list yet. She hasn't put in the years of ministry life like I have.* Immediately the Holy Spirit interrupted my thoughts. I felt Him whisper in my heart, "If I want her to become a *New York Times* bestseller, what is that to you? You do what I've called *you* to do! I love you just as much!" Wow! I felt such conviction! I spent the next few minutes confessing my envy to the Lord. Then I began to praise Him for what He is doing in my acquaintance's life. I asked God to expand her territory. I have discovered that the surest way to stop comparing is to start cheering.

WHAT DOES ENVY LOOK LIKE?

Here's the thing—envy is something we all wrestle with, but we must let go of comparing if we're going to be victorious. If we want God's blessing on our relationships, we've got to nix the idea that life is a competition. Yet, comparing has become a habit in so many lives.

Here are just a few scenarios to prove my point:

Cindy feels angry that her child didn't get the lead role in the school play. She feels the youth theater program is rigged.

Pam is annoyed that her son isn't on the starting lineup for the varsity basketball team. She complains that the school sports are political.

Sarah's been longing for a bigger house. The rising costs of housing, as well as interest rates, have kept her in a small, out-of-date home, which is much in need of remodeling. Then her friend Barb calls and invites her over to see her brand-new build with massive high ceilings and beautiful quartz countertops. Sarah goes because she is curious and wants to be a good friend, but when she gets there and sees it, she feels like she will be sick. From that time on, she backs away from Barb because it's too painful to be in such a beautiful home.

> *The possibilities for feelings of envy are endless.*

Professionally, Julie has been longing for a raise and promotion. Then she receives the excited phone call from her sister that *she* has received a huge promotion and pay raise. Julie feels like she can't sincerely celebrate because the longing in her own heart has been left unfulfilled. She hangs up quickly before she says something she'll regret, and she doesn't call her sister for the next month.

Leslie has been best friends with Sharlene for years. Then Sharlene receives an invitation to a concert for one of the biggest worship bands in the country by a new neighbor who's just moved in. Sharlene discovers she and her neighbor have lots in common and, as a result, she starts spending more time with her new acquaintance. Leslie feels nervous that her relationship with Sharlene is changing and she starts finding fault with Sharlene's new neighbor. Consciously or subconsciously, Leslie is trying to guard her friendship with Sharlene. However, she's going about it in the wrong way.

Brielle has been struggling to lose the weight from her recent pregnancy. It's felt so discouraging. Even as she's walked and nursed the past six months the scale is not moving much. Then Brielle goes on Instagram and sees a picture and post from her friend: "After only six weeks I'm back in my size two jeans!" Brielle slides down the pit of despair.

I asked a group of women what triggers envy in them the most and here were a few of their answers:

Social media posts
Comparing homes, kids, husbands
Someone else's success
For a single person—the desire for a spouse
Body image—another person's beauty

Ah, the possibilities for feelings of envy are endless. The problem is, rather than helping us find deeper connection with friends and loved ones, comparing often disconnects us from the people we long to be most connected with. As a result, we end up feeling lonelier.

Webster's Dictionary defines envy as the "painful or resentful awareness of an advantage enjoyed by another joined with a desire to possess the same advantage."[1] In the New Testament, the Greek word used for Envy is *phthonos* and is defined as "the feeling of displeasure produced by witnessing or hearing of the advantage or prosperity of others."[2] Envy is always rooted in comparing and this is why we must stop.

The Holy Spirit will never prompt you to become envious of others. In Paul's famous love chapter that we looked at in our chapter on giving up a fault-finding spirit, Paul writes that love "does not envy" (1 Cor.

> ***Our security needs to be first and foremost tied to God's unfailing love for us.***

13:4). James wrote some very harsh words to the early church such as, "For where you have envy and selfish ambition, there you find disorder and every evil practice" (James 3:16). Envy doesn't help the body of Christ, it creates division.

However, even though we want to love people, because we're human, envy is not likely to go away any time soon. When we feel rejected or as if we're not good enough, we begin comparing ourselves to others. But that is a recipe for disaster because comparison is rooted in insecurity. Our security needs to be first and foremost tied to God's unfailing love for us. When it's not, we want what others have because we imagine it will make us feel better about ourselves. Then we become envious, and jealousy left unchecked will ruin your relationships and leave you lonely. It destroys and divides.

We see this clearly in the tale of two sisters.

A TALE OF TWO SISTERS

Sisters are often the closest of friends. In fact, my own daughters are all very close as sisters. However, when envy enters the relationship, it divides the connection.

Do you remember Rachel and Leah from the Old Testament? Two sisters both ended up married to the same man. How do you think that turned out? Right?! Jacob worked seven years for Rachel because he loved her. However, Laban, Rachel's father, gave his older daughter, Leah, to marry Jacob first. As she would have been veiled during the ceremony, Jacob didn't discover it was Leah who was his wife until the morning after the wedding. Poor Leah must have kept her face covered all night. What a sad way to spend your honeymoon night!

When Jacob discovered he had been deceived, he was furious and decided to confront his father-in-law. Laban told Jacob he could marry Rachel after Leah had her wedding week, but he'd have to work for him another seven years for the privilege. (Not a great way to establish a close relationship with your son-in-law!) Jacob agreed and got to marry Rachel. However, with two wives, as you can imagine, things weren't so great within the family system.

Jacob's heart belonged to Rachel, which made Leah envious. Rachel had the very thing that Leah longed for: Jacob's love and attention. God felt compassion for Leah because she was unloved and He blessed her with children—lots of them (Gen. 29:31). Meanwhile, Rachel was barren. Leah had what Rachel wanted: kids! Women in this time in history had their worth measured by how many children they had. (That's messed up, right?) Rachel at one point went to Jacob in a fit of jealous rage and cried, "Give me children, or I'll die!" (Gen. 30:1).

If you follow the rest of the story through the book of Genesis, you will realize that the envy, rage, and dysfunction were passed down to the next generation. Leah's sons hated Rachel's son Joseph. In fact, if you remember, they sold him into slavery (Gen. 37:12–28).

I realize this story is extreme, but friends, hear me: comparison left unchecked moves to envy, and envy will ruin family systems and friendships alike. The result will be a deep loneliness. We must learn how to tame this ugly monster if we're going to experience the deep sense of community that God has designed us to enjoy.

We need the Holy Spirit's help for sure! In addition to allowing the Holy Spirit to search our hearts, we need to put some checks and balances in place to tame the envy monster.

HOW DO WE TAME THE MONSTER OF ENVY?

Here are some practical steps you can take to begin to get your jealousy under control. Before we look at those steps, be warned it is going to take some intentionality on your part and it's not always going to be easy. But the fact that it's not going to be easy will encourage you to press deeper into the power of the Holy Spirit, and that's a good thing! The first step is obvious but needs to be addressed.

Stop Comparing

Read that again out loud! Stop. Comparing.

Comparing creates competition in our hearts. The result is a lack of closeness in our relationships. You can't compete with your friends and expect to remain chummy. It simply doesn't work. Yet, it seems that if there is any common temptation for us women, comparing is it!

Those who aren't married compare their lot in life to those who are. Those who are married often feel discontent and compare their spouses to those of their friends. Others compare their bodies to those of other women. Many compare their homes to the homes of others. As women, we compare our gifts and talents, our achievements and even our kids. This is particularly true in the world of social media.

In her profound book *Killing Comparison,* author Nona Jones shares her own journey with comparing. Though she is an executive for Facebook and oversees faith-based partnerships for them, she talks in the book about the dangers for herself of scrolling through Instagram. At one point she realized there were people she needed to unfollow because they were stirring up envy in her. Wow! It would seem that the more a person scrolls through social media the more they long for someone else's life. The problem with constantly comparing is that we are stirring up more loneliness for ourselves, because when we grow envious, our natural tendency is to isolate.

Everyone is boasting about their platform these days and I really think God just shakes His head and rolls His eyes. The problem with platforms is that they encourage us to compete with others. Think about it. You scroll through Instagram and realize your friend has 40K followers. You have 300. You wish God would bless your Instagram account more. I mean why does your friend have all those followers? Friend, what if God doesn't care about social media platforms? Shocking, I know! What if what He truly desires is your heart and your deep contentment?

In another scenario, a group of pastors attend a conference together and start comparing how big their churches are. One pastor's church is growing off the charts. All of a sudden, the other pastors in the room are considering how to get their churches to grow. But here's the thing: we're not meant to compete with others in the body of Christ. We need to cultivate unity everywhere we can. Honestly, I don't believe God

For the sake of their friendship, they have made an agreement that they will not compete with each other.

will bring revival to a region until the church is unified in that area. Envy divides the church—it doesn't encourage unity.

I recently listened to a podcast with Katie Reid and Lee Nienhuis in which they were talking about their friendship. In the podcast they stated that they have a non-competitive agreement.[3] I love that! Katie and Lee both write books and are speakers. At times one may enjoy more success than the other. However, at the end of the day, they are both being used by God. For the sake of their friendship, they have made an agreement that they will not compete with each other. Instead, they'll cheer each other on!

I wonder whether we all need to "sign" non-compete forms with one another. We're all on the same team: Team Jesus. Let's rejoice with those who are experiencing the favor of the Lord. Some have greater gifts than others. That's a fact. But if we're going to enjoy deep friendship, we have to let go of comparing and competing.

This was the point of Jesus' teaching the parable of the workers in the vineyard (Matt. 20:1–16). In case you forgot that one, it's the story of a landowner who hires workers for his vineyard at different times throughout the day. Some work all day while others only work for an hour or so, yet they all get paid the same. If you have any sense of justice, you recognize that this isn't fair. Then the landowner, representing God, says, "Don't I have the right to do what I want with my own money?" Or to paraphrase for our purposes: "Don't I have the right to distribute gifts and callings as I wish?" Ah, that statement gives us pause, doesn't it?

Paul wrote, "We do not dare to classify or compare ourselves with some who commend themselves. When they measure themselves by themselves and compare themselves with themselves, they are not wise" (2 Cor. 10:12). Comparing is not wise. God has a unique story for you to live out (Eph. 2:10). When you start comparing your circumstances to those of others, you become competitive with your friends rather than cheering them on toward the calling God has given them. As a result, you're tempted to either criticize or back away from the friendship. Comparing and competing in friendship never ends well, so why not just stop?

Cultivate Continual Gratitude

According to a publication from Harvard Medical School, gratitude makes us happier. "Gratitude helps people feel more positive emotions, relish good experiences, improve their health, deal with adversity, and build strong relationships."[4] I also believe it makes us more content as well. If we constantly look at what we're lacking, we're going to feel a lot of discontent with our life. On the other hand, if we cultivate gratitude every day, we'll be more likely to have a positive and contented attitude.

Gratitude also contributes to deeper relationships and ultimately makes you a better friend. First of all, it makes you a more attractive friend to hang with. Cultivate gratitude and you'll find yourself shedding negativity and exuding a more positive attitude.

Expressing gratitude for your friends makes them feel more valued. Generally speaking, the more valued a person feels, the more invested in the relationship they will become. In your relationships, express how grateful you are for the people closest to you and your loneliness will decrease. Just the other day, I received a card with a handwritten note from a friend expressing how deeply grateful she was for our friendship. How do you think I felt after receiving that? Yup! I felt so loved and also inspired to be an even better friend. Rather than focusing on what might need work in the relationship, shift your focus to giving thanks for what's right about the relationship. I guarantee, just that tiny step will increase your connectedness and leave you feeling less lonely.

WORSHIP THE GIVER RATHER THAN THE GIFTS

We live in such a consumer-driven culture. Yet, the things we want can become idols in our lives. James, the brother of Jesus, reminds us that "every good and perfect gift is from above, coming down from the Father of the heavenly lights, who does not change like shifting shadows" (James 1:17). We are never invited to worship the gifts God gives. We are invited and instructed to worship the Giver of those gifts alone.

God gives a different measure of gifts to each person. All of them are to be used for His glory. Romans 12:6 reminds us that we have all been given different gifts according to God's grace.

None of us "own" those gifts. I am convinced that you will not be given a larger measure of authority and influence from the Lord until you crucify the tendency to be envious of others.

When I find myself jealous or envious of another's gifts, I get on my knees and bring my worship back to the Giver of the gifts. I praise Him that He alone knows what is best for my life and how He can best use me.

Practice Regular Fasting

Some believers seem to believe that fasting is not a discipline that needs to be practiced today. I disagree and believe that fasting is a necessary part of our prayer lives. Jesus said "when you fast," He didn't say "if you fast" (Matt. 6:16). Fasting curbs our appetites for lesser things and cleanses our souls from envy.

Fasting doesn't just include food. At times it can be more advantageous to fast from other things. For example, if you notice jealousy rising when you're looking at social media posts, fast from social media for a month. If you feel envious of your friend's material possessions, fast from spending for a month.

Become a Quick and Consistent Confessor

I have noticed that when I am quick to confess the first envious thought or thought of entitlement, the Holy Spirit not only cleanses me, but He also empowers me to be more grateful in the future. As I shared at the beginning of this chapter, the moment I compared myself to the very successful author whose book I saw in a bookstore, the Holy Spirit brought conviction and I confessed. Immediately, I gave thanks for the books God has allowed me to write. The more I confess and ask for His filling, the less I am tempted to become envious in the future.

Friend, far too often we have justified our envy as no big deal. When you become envious of a friend or loved one, it damages that relationship. However, that's not the only relationship it costs— envy also interrupts your connection to God. He has called us to be content (1 Tim. 6:6). If we're going to enjoy the deeply connected relationships that God has designed for us to experience, we're going to have to uproot envy. That means at the first envious thought, we stop. We pray, *Lord, forgive me. Cleanse me and restore to me a grateful spirit for all You've done in my life.*

Become an Enthusiastic Cheerleader

I was a cheerleader in college, and our job was to enthusiastically cheer for the soccer and basketball teams. In our friendships, we are to be each other's cheerleaders. I believe most people are dying for a little affirmation. Next time you find yourself comparing, confess and then cheer for your friend. Send them a note and let them know how happy you are for their accomplishment. I guarantee, it will quiet envy in your soul.

Pray the Lord's Prayer Every Day

Since I released *Our Father*,[5] a six-week Bible study on the Lord's prayer, I've been praying the Lord's prayer each day. It is such a great corrective for our envy because it reorders our world. When we pray "Our Father," we remember that God is our heavenly Father who is good and gives us good gifts. When we pray "Your kingdom come, Your will be done," we are reminded that it is about His kingdom and not our own. When we pray "forgive us our debts," we are reminded that we need daily forgiveness for our envious tendencies. When we pray the glorious benediction, "for Yours is the kingdom and the power and the glory forever," we are reminded that He gets all the glory and we are not to seek any kind of glory for ourselves.

My Father, I praise You that You are good and holy and just in all Your ways. You have been more than gracious to me by providing for my every need. Forgive me and cleanse me from any attitude of entitlement. Wash me and I will be as clean as fresh fallen snow. Precious Jesus, let me not take for granted the grace You have given me by envying the grace and gifts You've given others. Holy Spirit, I pray that You would fill me with gratitude for all You have done for me. Let thankfulness overflow from my heart. When I am tempted to become envious, help me, I pray, to shift my focus to Your goodness.

DIGGING DEEPER INTO CONNECTION

Deeper Connection with God

1. *Read Psalm 103 slowly out loud. The psalmist encourages us to remember all the Lord has done for us. Create a list of things you're thankful for and keep adding to it for a month. Remember all the blessings of the past few months. Then write a prayer of thanksgiving for how good He has been to you.*

2. *Read Luke 17:11–19. What tangible lesson is there in this story for your life? How might gratitude help you develop a deeper connection with God?*

3. *Read John 21:15–22. We are often concerned about the way God blesses others. Jesus reinstates Peter after Peter denied him. Then Jesus tells Peter he's not going to like the way he is going to die. Peter asks, "Lord, what about him?" speaking about John. What does this story teach you about comparing?*

Deeper Connection with Yourself

1. All of us are tempted to give in to comparison from time to time. Where are you most likely to fall into the comparison trap (e.g., your kids, your marriage, your work, body image)?

2. What would you say to your younger self about the pitfalls of comparison?

3. When you think back on different times in your life when you've felt rejected, how has that rejection affected your tendency to compare and envy?

4. Have you ever backed out of a friendship because you have sensed competition or you envy the other person?

Deeper Connection with Others

1. Who in your life struggles most with comparison and envy? How has that impacted you?

2. Which of your friends are able to truly celebrate victories with you? How has that contributed to your connection as friends?

3. This week, choose a friend who has something you long for and write them a note encouraging them and telling them how thankful you feel for their friendship.

God Doesn't Compare You to Another

"For you created my inmost being; you knit me together in my mother's womb. I praise you because I am fearfully and wonderfully made; your works are wonderful, I know that full well" (Ps. 139:13–14).

"Before I formed you in the womb I knew you, before you were born I set you apart" (Jer. 1:5).

"For just as each of us has one body with many members, and these members do not all have the same function, so in Christ we, though many, form one body, and each member belongs to all the others" (Rom. 12:4–5).

"But God has put the body together, giving greater honor to the parts that lacked it, so that there should be no division in the body, but that its parts should have equal concern for each other. If one part suffers, every part suffers with it; if one part is honored, every part rejoices with it" (1 Cor. 12:24b–26).

"For we are God's handiwork, created in Christ Jesus to do good works, which God prepared in advance for us to do" (Eph. 2:10).

LINDA'S STORY

Linda gets distracted, even a bit spacey at times. Once when we were together and she stopped for gas, she left the gas hose in her tank and started to pull away. We chuckled over that one. Another time, she pulled up to a bank drive-thru, which was right around the corner from Starbucks, and she ordered a Grande Dark Roast Coffee. The teller paused, then said, "Ma'am, this isn't Starbucks, it's First Bank." With Linda, I've had such delightful times of joy and laughter.

However, there is one area where Linda doesn't get distracted. In conversation she is fully present and listening intently when you pour out your heart to her. She's not checking her phone or looking over your shoulder when you're talking. She's not spacing out because she has other stuff on her mind. She's fully attentive. I know because I've experienced this. Linda has been a mentor in my life and has given me the gift of processing some of my most difficult challenges with her.

During an extremely rough season in my life, I often processed my thoughts and feelings with Linda. She would look me right in the eye as I processed, most of the time leaning toward me. Often, she would ask me questions inviting me to tell her more. Then she would invite me to my knees with her where we would pray together over the issues I had presented.

Linda is a treasure in my life because she has given me the gift of her full presence when we are together. I know she is like this with many friends and, as a result, is rarely lonely. Friends love to chat with Linda because they know that they have an attentive friend who will listen while they process. What a gift!

CHAPTER SIX

Be Attentive

*Value others above yourselves, not looking to your own interests
but each of you to the interests of the others.*

PHILIPPIANS 2:3–4

---

*Jesus is sometimes called Immanuel—"God with us." I think that's
what God had in mind, for Jesus to be present, to just be with us.
It's also what He has in mind for us when it comes to other people.*

BOB GOFF

Years ago, our family was vacationing in a beach community. Along the boardwalk there were lots of stores named Candy Kitchen. At the time our two youngest daughters were obsessed with Beanie Babies. If you were around in the 1990s you know what I mean. Beanie Babies were small stuffed animals that came with a name tag. It was quite the craze! It just so happened that all the Candy Kitchens along the boardwalk carried Beanie Babies.

One evening, we stopped in one so the girls could each purchase a Beanie Baby. Our son, around thirteen at the time, was fiddling with a suction cup ball mounted on the plexiglass container that held candy. He mindlessly fiddled with it until the unthinkable happened. It popped. What transpired next was a gigantic domino effect! Every plexiglass container toppled and hit another, which in turn hit another, and so on. Container after container tipped over. Thousands of candies spread far and wide through the store.

Seriously, it was epic! Jelly Bellies went rolling, chocolate balls went flying, caramels tumbled, and Swedish fish made a hard landing on the floor. Other customers stood with their mouths open and their eyes wide! No one could believe what had just happened. It was so shocking that I got the nervous giggles. My husband panicked and immediately offered to help clean up and pay for the lost candy. We apologized profusely. The store manager just pointed to the door and shouted in her most authoritative voice, "Get out!" Trust me, we left. I still laugh when I think back on that situation. I don't mean any disrespect toward those of you who run candy stores, but it was just so hilarious! But it's also a great reminder that **distraction creates disaster.**

Think about it.

Distracted drivers cause accidents.

Distracted hairdressers? Don't ask!

Distracted moms lose sight of their kids on the playground.

Distracted coworkers miss important meeting details.

Distracted spouses miss the clues that all is not well in the home.

The truth is, we've become the most distracted people in history and it's costing us in the relational department. We're missing out on deep connection in part because we've lost the ability to be fully present. As I write this, I can think of very few people who are attentive listeners. It's almost as if active, attentive listening is a lost skill. If we can't keep our focus completely on another person as they are sharing their heart, what kind of conversations can we really have? Conversations are key to deeper connection, so we must figure this out.

We are receiving numerous notifications on our phones daily. We have information and noise coming at us from every direction, and as a result our brains are scattered. With the barrage of information constantly assaulting our brains we've lost our capacity to focus for more than a few seconds. I read recently that the average attention span of an adult is 8.25 seconds.[1] Wowza! That is a shorter attention span

When was the last time you felt such deep connection with another person that your soul felt refreshed?

than a goldfish has! If that's true, we're in real trouble. But while these facts are interesting, we don't need research or studies to tell us that our relationships are struggling. We might be trying to be present, but our minds are spinning like tops with whirling information and ideas.

Let me ask you a few questions. You might need to pause and just consider for a moment. When was the last time you were fully focused, that is, completely present and undistracted while in conversation with another? When was the last time you felt such deep connection with another person that your soul felt refreshed? What if you could develop the habit of being more present, more attentive, less distracted? I'm guessing your life would be less stressed and more joyful. You'd be able to offer the calming presence of Christ to others. As a result, you would enjoy richer, more meaningful relationships. You'd feel more deeply connected and composed, less frantic and frazzled. You'd be able to live fully alive. Doesn't that sound wonderful? However, that means we have to get a bit more intentional about being fully present with others.

And honestly, you know what? God wants you to offer Him your full attention as well. It starts with Him and then flows out of us to others.

BE ATTENTIVE TO GOD

Do you remember the story of Martha and Mary? I can hear you groaning and thinking, *Isn't that the one where Martha gets a bad rap?* Don't worry, I'm not going to lay a guilt trip on you, but I do want to raise your awareness to what Jesus is really asking for in that story. In case you forgot, which I doubt, open your Bible and read the story found in Luke 10:38–42. I want you to notice *why* Jesus gently confronted Martha. Scripture says, "But Martha was *distracted* by all the preparations" (Luke 10:40; emphasis added). She was distracted. That might not seem like a big sin to you, but Jesus was concerned. Martha wasn't checking Pinterest for new recipes, she wasn't posting images on Instagram about how excited she was that Jesus was coming for dinner, and she wasn't checking her email or text messages. She didn't even have a smartphone. Yet, Jesus says that Martha missed what was best because she was distracted. What He wanted was her undivided attention. Mary, Martha's sister, gave Jesus her undivided attention, sitting at His feet to learn from Him, and that pleased Him. Our full presence is what He wants from us.

When was the last time you were able to sit attentively at the feet of Jesus, maybe to read His Word or to pray? You felt un-distracted. Your phone wasn't nearby begging to be checked. You simply were enjoying His presence. If that is a hard question for you to answer, try this. The next time you open your Bible put your phone in a completely different room. I'm trying this myself.

When we learn to be undistracted in the presence of Christ, I believe we will also be able to offer our undistracted attention to others. In this way, we'll be valuing others and living out Jesus' instructions to love the Lord our God with all our might and our neighbor as ourselves (Matt. 22:35–40).

The truth is when we love others, we offer our attentive ear. We lean in to listen in conversations.

OFFER YOUR ATTENTIVE EAR

Paul wrote to the believers in Philippi, "Do nothing out of selfish ambition or vain conceit. Rather, in humility value others above yourselves, not looking to your own interests but each of you to the interests of others" (Phil. 2:3–4). He goes on to write that we are to have the same attitude that Jesus had toward others (v. 5).

Think about it. Jesus treasured each person He met. He valued them and offered His full presence. He connected with people according to their interests and listened attentively to their hearts. With His disciples, He asked how their fishing was going and He used illustrations of fishing because many of them were fishermen by trade. When teaching people who knew about working the land, He used illustrations that they could relate to, like a farmer sowing seed. When He had individual conversations with people, such as the woman at the well (John 4:1–26), Nicodemus (John 3:1–21), or the rich young ruler (Mark 10:17–27), he offered each person His full presence as He listened. He asked insightful questions to keep them talking.

I remember a pivotal time when I asked my daughter how she viewed me as a listener. I was expecting rave reviews, but I received very different feedback. I wrote about it in my book *How to Listen So People Will Talk*. Bethany's reflections on my listening ability showed me that I had a very long way to go in order to be the listener I wanted to be. I wanted my daughter to feel loved and that meant she needed to feel heard. That conversation was a wake-up call for me. I realized I needed God's help to be the attentive, fully present listener He was calling me to be. As a result, I began working on my listening skills, such as not interrupting, asking great questions, staying focused, and letting go of distractions.

I don't want to miss what's best as far as enjoying my relationships with Jesus and others because I'm distracted. I'm guessing you don't either, but that means we need to figure out what's distracting us and make some changes. Jesus' desire is for us to be *fully* present so we feel connected.

In order to make those necessary changes, let's look at some of our top distractions as far as relationships.

SOME TOP DISTRACTIONS

Technology

You knew I was going to say that, didn't you? Technology is a gift, yet because we are constantly texting, checking social media, and emailing on our phones, we're more distracted than ever. As I alluded to earlier in the chapter, the constant barrage of information is robbing us of our capacity to focus. With the invention of the smartphone, we all of a sudden became accessible to others 24/7 and we're addicted to the constant stimulation. The problem is our brains have lost the ability to concentrate for much longer than eight seconds.

When studying how our addiction to our phones is influencing our relationships, I learned about "phubbing." This is when you're with someone but you are snubbing or ignoring them in favor of spending time on your phone.[2] We've all experienced this. I talked with an acquaintance I met at a conference who told me that her friend was texting with others the entire time they were together at lunch. Don't be guilty of doing the same. Stop phubbing people! Next time you're out to lunch with a friend, put your phone away. But you might be wondering, what about when I'm not with another person and just feel like vegging out with my phone? Great question!

When we've been ruminating on a problem for a while, we often want the numbing effect of scrolling through Facebook, Instagram, YouTube, or X, so we don't have to think. However, be warned. Dr. Gregory Jantz writes, "Perhaps the most ironic modern-day cause of withdrawal, isolation and even depression comes via social media." He adds, "If social media acts as a substitute for in-person relationships, a person's sense of isolation and inadequacy can worsen."[3] There is a distinct link between how much time a person spends on social media and how lonely they feel.

So what do we do? Social media is not going away anytime soon. Harvard Health suggests limiting social media interaction to thirty minutes per day, citing a study that says this guideline "may lead to significant improvement in well-being."[4] When you exceed that, you're liable to feel lonely and depressed. Why? Because, as I've mentioned earlier, we were designed for community as humans created in the image of a relational God. We need to strengthen our ability to focus on others and be fully present to them. That means we need to limit the time we spend scrolling.

Busy Schedules

Our schedules are pulling us at a hectic pace and leaving us frantic and frazzled, with little emotional energy for friendships. As a result, we're distracted from what matters most. The drive to achieve and live a successful life has translated to living a rushed, overcommitted life. But the constant static of underlying hurry is robbing us of deep connection.

Being busy saps our energy because it drains our emotional and physical capacity to keep up with life's nonstop demands. As a result, we become too tired for people. In *The Ruthless Elimination of Hurry*, John Mark Comer warns against a busy lifestyle that leads to weak relationships, disconnection from God, poor health, and overall feeling of lack of purpose.[5] I remember reading Comer's book and being profoundly struck with how easy it is to get sucked back into the vortex of busyness. We must guard against it if we are going to enjoy our connection with Jesus and others. Think about it—Jesus valued each person He encountered. We need to follow His example. If we are willing to create more space in our schedules, we will reap the benefit of more connected friendships.

Worries and Concerns

With the rise of anxiety and fear, many have lost control of the myriad of thoughts racing through their minds. As a result, they are unable to engage and concentrate fully in conversations with others. Our worries and fears are cluttering our minds and exhausting our ability to connect. Ultimately it is leading to deeper loneliness, which in turn is creating more anxiety. What a vicious cycle!

We need a plan. Rather than beating yourself up over your worries, I suggest in my devotional, *Psalms for the Anxious Heart*, that you learn to turn your panic into praise.[6] The more you practice the easier it will become, and the more space you will free up in your thinking to focus on others. In addition to turning your panic into praise, here are some questions to consider:

What worries take up the most space in your thinking? Are there concerns you need to leave at the feet of Jesus? Do you need to talk with a Christian therapist about the amount of anxiety you are experiencing? Have you talked with your medical doctor about whether or not an anti-anxiety medication would be beneficial? These are all good questions to consider if worry is beginning to damage your relationships.

TO BECOME MORE ATTENTIVE

Slow Down and Embrace Transition Time

If we're going to value our relationships and be attentive, we've got to slow down. Embrace transition time. Leave space between appointments. Leave a few minutes earlier to pick up your kids from school so that you aren't driving like a maniac and unable to focus on their needs by the time they get in the car. When you're headed to an appointment, leave five minutes earlier than you need so that you can spend a few minutes praying beforehand that God will help you offer your full presence. On your way home from work, ask the Holy Spirit to help you let go of work concerns so that you can be fully invested and undistracted with those you love.

Letting go of hurry is going to take practice because most of us are addicted to hurry. Embracing transition time will definitely help. God is calling us to relax and enjoy people. It's absolutely shocking to realize, but Jesus was never in a hurry! He never turned to the disciples and shouted, "Get your sandals on, we're running late!" Instead, He was purposeful and allowed Himself to be interrupted by others, giving them His full attention.

Create Quiet Space in Your Day

No matter how extroverted we might be, we do need to quiet ourselves to be present to Christ and to reorder our lives around His agenda. We need a detox from all the noise in our heads. Simply put, His agenda prioritzes people and loving them well. In order to love and connect with people as Jesus did, we need to be spending time with Jesus so that we are transformed in His presence. His heart must become ours. How can we hear the quiet voice of His Spirit if we're never quiet? In order to enjoy your relationship with God and to gain His heart for people, you need times of quiet to listen, reflect, and read His Word.

In addition to listening to God, our brains need quiet to recalibrate. *Time* magazine reported that in 1859, "Florence Nightingale wrote that: 'Unnecessary noise, then, is the most cruel absence of care which can be inflicted either on sick or well.'" The article went on to say that "'trying to hear in silence' can demonstrably accelerate the growth of valuable brain cells. This act of listening to quiet can, in itself, enrich our capacity to think and perceive."[7]

It makes sense that embracing quiet can help us focus more during conversations and give us greater ability to perceive and understand what the other person is saying. As a result, the person feels heard and valued, and we end up feeling more connected.

Put Your Phone Away

We need a detox from the addiction of our phones. By taking clean breaks from technology each day—for example, put your phone away for at least thirty minutes each day—we'll recondition our brains to center more attentively on the people we love.

Rather than constantly being accessible, set boundaries and choose specific times during the day to answer email. Put your phone away during dinner time so that you can enjoy conversations happening around the table. Set your phone on "Do Not Disturb" so that you can be present with your family in the evening, and then later to get a good night's rest.

Cultivate Curiosity

Each person created by God is a masterpiece and worth knowing. One of the most practical ways I know to be attentive is to simply cultivate curiosity when you're having conversations. Curiosity says, "Tell me more. I'm *interested* in learning more." The more curious you are, the less likely you are to become distracted when someone is telling you something about their life.

Heather Holleman, in her intriguing book *The Six Conversations*, writes, "If I could pick one essential character trait for my children and students to develop, I'd choose that of curiosity." She goes on to describe interpersonal curiosity as "the desire to know and understand more about other people."[8] If we're going to feel more connected and less lonely, we've got to practice the skill of interpersonal curiosity.

Learn to ask questions and invite others to tell you more. Remind yourself of Paul's instructions to "in humility value others above yourselves, not looking to your own interests but each of you to the interests of others" (Phil. 2:3b–4). Part of valuing another person is taking a genuine interest in that person and cultivating curiosity to know more.

Friend, the truth is if we are going to live less lonely lives and connect more deeply, we need to learn to be attentive. It will take some intentionality and perhaps a bit of inconvenience as we let go of distractions, but in the long run it will be so worth the effort.

> *Lord Jesus, I long to be attentive to both You and others. Yet, so often I find myself distracted. I'm a whole lot more like Martha than Mary. Change me, Holy Spirit. Develop in me a heart that desires to be fully focused in Your presence. Lord, I realize after reading this chapter that if I am going to enjoy deeper connections with others, I need to eliminate some distractions so that I can bring my full self to conversations. Teach me how to listen attentively so that each person I am with feels treasured and valued.*

DIGGING DEEPER INTO CONNECTION

Deeper Connection with God

1. *Read Psalm 46:10 slowly out loud. Then practice being absolutely silent and still for five minutes. Visualize Jesus sitting right next to you. What do you think He would say to you?*

2. *Read Luke 10:38–42. Replace Martha's name with yours and imagine Jesus saying that you are distracted. Then spend a few moments writing down what is distracting you these days. Open your hands and give every distraction to God. Then tell Him you're ready to give Him your undivided attention.*

Deeper Connection with Yourself

1. *What most often distracts you when you're in conversations with others? What tangible steps could you take to be more attentive in those conversations?*

2. *Do you ever find yourself mindlessly scrolling through social media posts when you feel bored? What might be a better activity that makes space for you to build deeper connections?*

Deeper Connection with Others

1. *Put your phone away whenever you are at coffee, lunch, or simply in a conversation with a friend. Give that person your undivided attention. Look at them while they're talking and lean in. Your body language says a lot about how attentive you are.*

2. *On the way to the next lunch you schedule with a friend, think of five questions you could ask based on the last time you were together. For instance, if the last time you were together they talked about a struggle at their job, ask them how it's going. Or if they shared about a concern with one of their kids, ask for an update.*

3. *Think through some of the people closest to you. Write down a list of the top things that interest them. Part of being attentive to another is learning about their interests.*

God Is Attentive to You

"The LORD hears the needy and does not despise his captive people" (Ps. 69:33).

"Before they call I will answer; while they are still speaking I will hear" (Isa. 65:24).

"Are not five sparrows sold for two pennies? Yet not one of them is forgotten by God. Indeed, the very hairs of your head are all numbered" (Luke 12:6–7).

"For the eyes of the Lord are on the righteous and his ears are attentive to their prayer" (1 Peter 3:12).

ASHLEY'S STORY

Ashley was crushed. For the seventh time in five years, the doctor was saying, "I'm so sorry Ashley, but the baby is gone."

The familiar feeling of emptiness washed over her whole body. Every hope, dream, and desire for her baby's life melted away.

Through sobs, she wrestled in prayer. "How can this be happening again? Why did my body fail this baby? What's wrong with me? How am I going to recover from this again? Am I not a good enough mom to be entrusted with another life? What did I miss? Why does this keep happening?" Out of the darkness of despair, she prayed, "Please God, don't let this pain and suffering go to waste. Show me what You want me to do with this."

Then she remembered something she had shared with some women from church: the incredible and unexplainable value of being vulnerable with your safe people. The people you have invested deep relationships with inside of your community. Even though miscarriages can feel incredibly private, Ashley reminded herself how imperative it was to allow people in and allow them to love and comfort you through the hard times. Yet this time, she felt she just couldn't bear the burden of knowing the sadness and disappointment the miscarriage would cause others.

Thankfully, the Holy Spirit reminded her that isolation wouldn't help. The most life-giving choice would be to let others in. So Ashley shared with her trusted community. They spoke life and truth into her heart. They reminded her of who she was and who God created her to be. They didn't minimize her pain. They grieved with her and supported her. As a result, Ashely felt the beautiful connection of true community.

CHAPTER SEVEN

Offer and Receive Comfort

Comfort one another.

2 CORINTHIANS 13:11 ESV

When we are temporarily overburdened due to the stress of death, divorce, illness, and so on, we definitely need the supportive help of our sisters. We need someone to come alongside us and help shoulder the overburden.

DEE BRESTIN

The Italian Renaissance artist Michelangelo sculpted a masterpiece that now sits in Saint Peter's Basilica. The *Pietà* is a statue of Mary, the mother of Jesus, cradling the broken body of her Son after it was removed from the cross.

You might remember the bombing of the Alfred Murrah federal building in Oklahoma City in 1995 that took the lives of 168 people, including nineteen children. Even if you don't remember the event, you've likely seen the poignant photo of a firefighter cradling the body of a small child. The author of an article about the tragedy dubbed the image the "pietà" sentiment.[1]

I am convinced that one of the reasons we experience so much loneliness is that we have forgotten the pietà sentiment. We have forgotten how to hold and comfort one another in life's sorrows as the broken body of Christ. We were not designed to carry our pain alone. We need each other in our seasons of sorrow and suffering.

My dear friend and mentor Linda lost her adult daughter to liver cancer. Grief and sorrow have come in wave after wave. In one conversation I had with Linda, she made the comment that often people don't know how to comfort those who are walking through grief and sorrow. Grief makes us nervous. I couldn't agree more!

I have felt those feelings when desiring to comfort someone in their pain. I would hope that by my actions or words I could lighten the load of sorrow for them. But at times I grow paralyzed. I've felt the angst that I would say the wrong thing. Perhaps it's the same for you. Part of healing our loneliness is learning how to comfort others in their sorrow and being willing to receive the comfort of others in our own sorrow.

HOW DO WE DEFINE COMFORT?

When we look into the New Testament meaning of the word comfort, we find that various forms of the word are used. The Greek word for comfort often means "a calling to one's side." Sometimes it's used to "combine encouragement with alleviation of grief."[2] This is how it is used by Paul in 2 Corinthians 13:11 where he exhorts us to comfort one another.[3] The idea is that when someone is walking through sorrow and grief, we are to come alongside them to encourage them and alleviate their grief in any way humanly possible.

While that's clarifying for us, it's also where we sometimes get into trouble. Let me explain.

While we can and should come alongside others in their grief, we cannot fix or take away their grief. We can, however, alleviate their pain by being physically present with them, listening attentively, and offering practical forms of service. We can also allow others to listen to us in our pain and sit with us while we process. Jesus not only comforted others but also welcomed and hoped that others would comfort Him.

JESUS OFFERED COMFORT
EVERYWHERE HE WENT

Remember the story of Lazarus? When Jesus arrived, Lazarus had been dead for several days. His sisters, Mary and Martha, were in the depths of grief. The sisters both said to Jesus, "If only you had been here." Their hearts were wrenched and wrung dry from all the tears they had shed. When Mary fell at Jesus' feet sobbing, Scripture tells us that Jesus was so moved by compassion that He Himself wept (John 11:35). Did you get that? The one who created the sun, moon, and stars cried. Imagine that!

The Almighty stood with tears streaming down His face because He had entered so fully into His friends' sorrow. What's shocking is Jesus knew the end of the story. He knew that momentarily He would raise Lazarus from the dead, yet He offered visible empathy to his precious friends Mary and Martha. What a picture of tangible comfort.

In another New Testament story Jesus comforts a widow. You can read about it in Luke 7:11–16. Jesus entered the town of Nain and saw a funeral procession leaving town. The young man who died was the only son of a widow. Imagine her grief! She had lost her husband to death and now lost her only son.

When Jesus saw her, His heart was filled with compassion and He moved close to her. With incredible tenderness He whispered, "Don't cry!" Then Jesus moved to the bier the pallbearers were carrying and told the dead young man to get up. Immediately, the dead son came back to life, sat up, and began talking! Jesus not only moved close to the woman to offer His presence, but He alleviated her suffering by raising her son back to life.

The Holy Spirit may bring thoughts of hope to us as we're praying, and He may bring tangible comfort through the arms of a friend or family member.

There's so much I love about this story! I especially love the tenderness of Jesus. He continually brings comfort by offering both His presence and His power in our times of sorrow. When life falls apart, we may fear that Christ's comfort is not available. Oh friend, that is not true! Scripture teaches us that before Jesus left to return to heaven, He told the disciples that He was going to leave the Comforter with them (John 14:15–18). The Comforter, referring to the Holy Spirit (also called the Advocate and Helper), would be with us and in us! The Spirit of Jesus is our 24/7 companion and source of continual comfort.

How does the Holy Spirit comfort us? He may remind us

of a Scripture we've memorized, or He may bring a song to mind that has ministered to us in the past. He may bring thoughts of hope to us as we're praying, and He may bring tangible comfort through the arms of a friend or family member. The question that begs to be asked at this point is, are we willing to allow the Holy Spirit to use others to comfort us? Many times we may feel private about our personal sorrows. That's understandable. However, we need to have some trusted people in our lives with whom we are real. If we don't, we're going to feel lonely. That requires vulnerability. We see this in the life of Christ.

Remember when Jesus was praying in the Garden of Gethsemane? He was in dark despair as He thought ahead to the coming torture of the cross. In that moment He desperately wanted the disciples to stay awake and be in the pain with Him. He longed for the comfort of His friends (Matt. 26:38–40). Some of us are good at comforting others but we're not so great at receiving comfort ourselves. Have you ever had a friend who always tried to be "the strong one"? As a result, something felt lacking in the friendship. God's plan for us in the body of Christ is that we give and *receive* comfort.

Sometimes it's easier to give comfort than to ask for it or receive it. We just don't want to be a burden to someone else. We don't want to be a "Debbie Downer," so we isolate. However, the problem is that in true friendship, comfort goes both ways. We give comfort *and* we receive comfort. If you worry about being a burden to others, I suggest that you spend some time asking God to heal that concern. As we just saw, Jesus needed comfort from His friends. Though He was King of kings and Lord of lords, He was willing to make His needs known in the garden. We need to follow Christ's humble example and allow ourselves to be comforted by others.

WHY MIGHT WE WITHHOLD COMFORT?

I've been mulling this over in my mind and asking the Holy Spirit to show me why we don't comfort one another more effectively. We want to offer comfort and we also want to receive comfort. So then, what's the problem? Good question. I think there are several problems.

Compassion Fatigue

What is compassion fatigue? I would describe it as being overwhelmed with the number of problems surrounding us, which causes us to shut down some of our emotions. When compassion fatigue sets in, we become indifferent to protect our hearts. Let me give you a few examples.

When Steve and I were living in Sudan in the early 1980s, we saw so many beggars. They lined the streets. Many had broken bodies or other special needs. I wanted to help them all. I felt overwhelmed by their sorrow and the way they were disregarded by society. However, in the years we were there, I noticed an alarming shift in myself. I noticed that when I walked down the street, I no longer wanted to look at those people. At times, I even felt the need to cover my ears to block out their cries for help. Now, to be clear I didn't do that, but that's what I felt like. I felt as though my senses couldn't take in any more suffering. I had compassion fatigue. I had dumbed down my emotions to survive. When we arrived home from the mission field, I remember spending extended times with the Lord asking Him to heal my heart and reignite tenderness in me because I wanted to be like Him. I wanted to be able to weep over the things that He wept over.

Similarly, a friend recently told me that she had heard so many stories of cancer recently, she felt as though if she heard one more story she would scream. She wanted to cover her ears and not hear another word about cancer. I understand.

Another young friend told me she needed a break from social media because she saw so many stories of those who were hurting that her soul needed a rest.

What do we do with compassion fatigue? We know that Jesus calls us to be kind and empathic with those who are suffering, so how do we solve this problem? We must understand and embrace our limits. In today's world, thanks to the internet, we have the potential to stay in touch and hear stories from thousands and thousands of people. We see graphic pictures of suffering from all around the world on the news. We need to limit what we view and who we comfort. It's not possible with our physical and emotional limitations to comfort everyone. When we try to do that, we end up with compassion fatigue.

According to British psychologist and anthropologist Robin Dunbar, humans are only cognitively able to maintain about 150 connections at once.[4] Your inner circle can only include approximately five close friends. Think about the world of social media where some of us have 5,000 "friends" on Facebook and thousands following us on Instagram. While we can encourage others on

> *What do we do with compassion fatigue? We must embrace our limits in order to be the compassionate, comforting people God has called us to be.*

those platforms, we cannot possibly maintain all those relationships without becoming exhausted. And it's certainly not possible to comfort them all. We must embrace our limits in order to be the compassionate, comforting people God has called us to be.

Busyness

Part of the reason we are so exhausted is because we are so busy. It is also what keeps us from comforting others and even receiving comfort ourselves. We mean well, it's just that we have so many places to go and people to see that the friends who are grieving are often left behind. We may assume that they want space when in reality they might just want a friend to sit and cry with them. We may have time to send a card or drop off flowers, but then the next appointment calls. As a result, journeying with someone through the long haul of grief can feel overwhelming.

We even run from our own sorrow in an attempt to escape the pain. Rather than sitting with our disappointment or grief, we simply pack our schedules and keep going. The problem is, pain that is not grieved comes out in other ways. We might snap at our spouse or kids. We might develop stomach ulcers or indigestion. What if we slowed down and lived at a pace that created room for pain and heartbreak? I believe we would be more emotionally and spiritually healthy and enjoy more connected relationships if we created the space for grieving.

Being Uncomfortable with Pain

Some of us, because of our personality types, are just plain old uncomfortable with pain and suffering. We see ourselves as "the positive people." Suffering makes us nervous. When we're with a friend who is hurting, we try to empathize, but we much prefer to move on to happier topics. As a result, we try to fix the other person's pain. We try to make it better. However, in our attempts we actually make things worse. We might throw in a quick positive thought or a Band-Aid Scripture, which makes our friend feel like we haven't really entered into their pain. Or we might say, "I understand" when in reality we don't understand. What if we asked the Man of Sorrows, Jesus, to create in us a deeper understanding of how God uses pain? What if we really believed His statement "Blessed are those who mourn" (Matt. 5:4)?

Once we realize our hang-ups, we're more equipped to move forward with developing some healthy comforting habits.

BEST PRACTICES FOR OFFERING COMFORT TO OTHERS

First let's look at a few "don'ts." Then, we'll consider some helpful "dos."

A FEW DON'TS

Don't Use Pious Christian Platitudes

When someone is in deep pain or grief, don't quote Scripture to them or offer short sermons designed to fix the situation. Author Dee Brestin in *The Friendships of Women* describes the pain of receiving pious platitudes in cards after her husband, Steve, died. Dee wrote, "Even condolence cards can twist a knife by giving you a little sermonette. When my husband was dying and suffering incredibly, I'd open up a card that said, 'All things work together for the good

119

of those who love God and are called according to His purpose.' And I'd want to scream, '*How insensitive!*' I know the verse is true, but there is a time to speak it, and a time to be silent. High-tide grief calls for empathy, *not* solutions."[5] The lesson for you and me is to not throw a Bible verse at someone's horrific sorrow and assume we've helped.

Don't Say, "I understand" or "I know how you feel"

The truth is you can't fully understand another person's pain because each person's story is different. Don't assume you know how the person feels, because they might be so overwhelmed with grief that they don't even know how they feel.

When someone is in deep grief, the greatest gift to them might be your quiet presence. No words. Just your presence and your tears. If you do say something, make your focus validating what they're feeling. You might say something like, "I can't imagine how much pain you're in right now!"

Don't Say Vaguely, "Let me know what I can do"

The suffering person may not know what they need. They might feel weird asking for help. Instead, ask God for a practical idea to help. You might order them dinner. My friend Danita, who lost her husband tragically and unexpectedly, suggests buying paper products like: paper plates, plastic cutlery, toilet paper, water bottles, and tissues. Danita also suggests offering "to drive your grieving friend to appointments or to drive their kids to school."[6]

HELPFUL "DOS"

Do Run Errands for the Person Grieving

You can ask, "What errands can I run for you today?" Think practical. Perhaps you can make a grocery run or pick up a prescription. Ask what items they might need and then offer to go get them. Perhaps offer to pick up their kids from school or take them to soccer practice and pick them up. For a widow or a friend recently divorced, you could offer to take her car and have the oil changed. Often being relieved of small errands brings the most comfort.

Similarly, do offer to go with the grieving person to an appointment that could be overwhelming. Often when a person is grieving, attending to administrative details feels staggering. Having someone alongside who can help listen and plan can be a great assistance.

Do Deliver Small Gifts

Perhaps the one suffering just needs a cup of coffee from their favorite coffee shop. It's amazing how it can boost someone's spirits to receive a latte or Americano on a bleak day. Perhaps you can fill a basket with goodies and drop it at their house. Or you could bring some flowers or a plant. Any little gift can raise a person's spirits.

I remember when one of my daughters miscarried. She was absolutely devastated. We all were. A friend of hers dropped off a drink from her favorite coffee shop and a beautiful dainty necklace to remember the sweet baby my daughter would not deliver.

Ruth was devastated when she lost her sister to cancer. Her sister had loved flower gardens. Ruth's friend knew how deeply she was grieving and so she ordered a special necklace designed with a beautiful flower. Every time the tears begin to flow, Ruth can feel the necklace and remember what a treasure her sister was.

Recently, my father-in-law who we loved dearly, died at age ninety-four. Even though we knew his death was imminent, we experienced grief. Unexpectedly, we received a beautiful card simply written about the willingness to listen to our stories and our grief. What a comfort!

Do Offer to Pray but Also Write Out Your Prayer

At times the grief is so profound that the person grieving may not want you to pray with them in person. However, they will likely be open to your praying for them. Send a notecard with a prayer written out or text or email the words of your prayer for them. There is nothing as sweet as a handwritten card.

Do Offer to Give a Hug or Arrange for a Massage

I love to give and receive hugs, but I have learned to ask. Some people don't appreciate being touched at all when they're grieving. Others feel comforted by a hug.

The week before my father-in-law died, he was in a great deal of pain. At one point, I asked him, "Dad, what can I do for you? How can I help?" He paused a minute and then he said, "Becky, just hug me." I gathered his frail, bony body in my arms and held him close. I whispered in his ear, "Dad, I love you. You're precious to me." He replied in a soft voice, "I love you dearly, Becky." During that little exchange, he was comforted as he was grieving, his body starting to decay, and I was comforted as I knew soon I would lose this dear man of God in my life.

I read recently that one of the practices used by hospice houses during the 1990s was called the "hospice hold."[7] I honestly don't know if this is still practiced today, but apparently at times the hospice care worker would crawl onto the bed to hold the dying person. As the person passed from one life to another, the hug they experienced comforted them.

Do Deliver a Meal or Set Up a Meal Train

Meal trains are great because they give friends something tangible to do for the person grieving. There are several meal delivery services that can be so helpful in terms of grief. Grief tends to cloud our ability to think and plan, so delivering a meal to a friend eliminates one less task the person has to do. Especially when a loved one has died, the administrative side of things is overwhelming. Delivered meals can be such a blessing.

Do Ask the Comforter Himself to Fill You

One night during the writing of this chapter, I was lying in bed, thinking about this chapter and praying. Like you, I haven't always comforted others well. Sometimes, I've really messed it up, saying the wrong thing or not being there when my friends needed me because I had other commitments. My intentions have been good in the sense that I truly desired to help. As I was thinking, the Lord reminded me that I have the Holy Spirit living within me. Once again, I realized how imperative it is that we ask Him to fill us. If He fills us with Himself, His comfort will flow out of our lives to others. That's what I want, don't you? In light of that, I thought it would be fitting to close this chapter with a prayer to be filled with the Holy Spirit. Once we have received Christ, the Holy Spirit dwells within us. However, we need to continually be refilled, giving more and more of ourselves to His lordship. Let's take a moment and pray this prayer.

Holy Spirit, more and more I realize how much I need You to refill me. Many people who are in my life need comfort. Life is disappointing. Some are grieving big losses and others seemingly small ones, but almost everyone around me needs comfort. I long to offer them the comfort that is so characteristic of You. Fill me now, I pray, Holy Spirit, so that your love and comfort flow from my life to others.

DIGGING DEEPER INTO CONNECTION

Deeper Connection with God

Read and write out 2 Corinthians 1:3–4.

1. *What do these verses teach you about God's comfort?*

2. *What do these verses teach you about God's desire for you to comfort others?*

3. *At times, Christians have taken these verses to mean that when someone is grieving, they should plunge in with their own story of grieving to comfort their friends. Why is this not a great idea?*

4. *Read Isaiah 51:12. How is God described in this verse?*

5. *Read Psalm 147:3. What does this teach you about God's heart for the hurting?*

Deeper Connection with Yourself

1. When others are deeply hurting and in a place of grief, how do you most often try to comfort them?

2. What mistakes have you made when trying to comfort someone? Don't dwell on these, but do ask the Holy Spirit to give you wisdom in the future.

3. When a friend experiences a death in their family, do you encounter anxiety over figuring out the right thing to say? What tangible ideas do you have after reading this chapter that might help you bring comfort to someone who is grieving?

Deeper Connection with Others

1. The next time you are in a conversation with someone who is grieving, try saying less. Sit with the person in silence. Instead of trying to fix their sorrow, invite them to tell you more about their loved one. Listen attentively.

2. Ask some of your closest friends how they feel most comforted when they are grieving. Grieving doesn't always involve the death of a loved one. At times, your friend might be grieving a lost opportunity or a disappointment at work. In order to be a more comforting friend, it's good to ask ahead what helps your friend feel the most comfort when they're in the midst of disappointing circumstances.

God Offers Comfort

"Blessed are those who mourn, for they will be comforted"
(Matt. 5:4).

"Yet I am always with you; you hold me by my right hand. You
guide me with your counsel, and afterward you will take me into
glory" (Ps. 73:23–24).

"He heals the brokenhearted and binds up their wounds"
(Ps. 147:3).

"Whoever dwells in the shelter of the Most High will rest in the
shadow of the Almighty. I will say of the LORD, 'He is my refuge
and my fortress, my God, in whom I trust'" (Ps. 91:1–2).

"He will wipe every tear from their eyes. There will be no more
death or mourning or crying or pain, for the old order of things
has passed away" (Rev. 21:4).

MELODIE'S STORY

I'll let Melodie tell you her story in her own words:

"My husband, Todd, and I retired in Prescott, Arizona, at the end of the summer season. While Prescott is a friendly town, starting over at this point in life was not easy. We were meeting people and making acquaintances but struggling with true connection. We figured soon we would find a church and get plugged in. However, what we didn't plan on was the tragic death of our youngest son. I was devastated beyond words and withdrew.

"At first, I welcomed the social isolation. No questions to answer, no looks of pity to endure, no drop-in visitors to manage as I was grieving. However, after a few months, the Lord began to help me see it was time to take initiative and engage. We found a church and I met some wonderful women there. They welcomed me in without hesitation. As I began to share details of my story with this new group of friends, they prayed with me and for me. They showed me kindness and grace. They practiced hospitality, feeding my soul in a way the best casserole or home-cooked meal could not. They offered me the welcome mat of friendship and connection and helped me experience the joy of laughter once more.

"Prior to this, I always thought hospitality meant inviting someone into my home, preparing and sharing a meal, and being a gracious hostess. My new circle of friends gave me a new perspective. They showed me the hospitality of the heart. They welcomed me into their circle. I will be forever grateful."

CHAPTER EIGHT

Open Your Heart *and* Your Home

Offer hospitality to one another without grumbling.

1 Peter 4:9

Those who live out radically ordinary hospitality see their homes not as theirs at all but as God's gift to use for the furtherance of his kingdom. They open doors; they seek out the underprivileged. They know that the gospel comes with a house key.

Rosaria Butterfield

What comes to mind when you hear the word "hospitality"? Glossy magazines such as *Magnolia* and *Victoria* and *Better Homes and Gardens*? Beautifully decorated tables and elaborate menus? Fresh cut flowers atop a gleaming table with sun pouring through streak-free windows? Dressed-up guests?

Or is it that person from church who offers to host meetings in her small living room? The person whose house is always filled with neighbors' children, all of whom are allowed to make noise and be themselves? The one who can't have company over but who brings her offering of baked goods to a gathering?

In God's eyes, the closest word to hospitality would be "welcome." Recently, I bought a new welcome mat for my front porch. The old one was ratty and dirty, and I felt embarrassed whenever anyone came to my home. The first person to notice my new welcome mat was my sweet grandson Noah. He said, excitedly, "You got a new welcome mat, Mimi!" I loved his enthusiasm. I want those who come to my home to feel warmly welcomed. After hearing Noah's admiration, I began to pray that others would feel immediately welcomed by me—welcomed in my heart and in my home. That is the essence of hospitality.

Hospitality is making someone feel welcomed;
opening your home and your heart.

HOSPITALITY WAS GOD'S IDEA

Hospitality was God's idea. The Greek word *oikos* meaning "home, house or household" was used over 180 times in the New Testament.[1] To the early church, hospitality was the norm. It was part of being a follower of Jesus. If you followed Christ, you opened your heart and your home. There were no church buildings at the time, so small communities of believers met in homes.

Luke writes in the book of Acts that "all the believers were together and had everything in common" (Acts 2:44). Peter instructed the early church to "offer hospitality to one another without grumbling" (1 Peter 4:9). Paul reminds us to "practice hospitality" (Rom. 12:13). Jesus Himself spent quite a bit of time at the home of Mary and Martha of Bethany (Luke 10:38–42). Friends, God's desire is for us to welcome others into our homes and our hearts.

Hospitality was a core value of the early church. It was one of the defining marks of the followers of the Way. Flavius Claudius Julianus (Julian the Apostate), the Roman Emperor from 361–363, referred to Christian charity as a model for the Roman philanthropic system. "These impious Galileans [Christians] not only feed their own poor, but ours also; welcoming them into their *agapae*, they attract them, as children are attracted, with cakes."[2]

Sharing a meal together and breaking bread together were a joy for the early church. Without hotels as we think of today, traveling ministers and friends would stay in homes with other believers, eating with the family and enjoying deep spiritual conversations around the table. It wasn't until the fourth century that hotels and hospitals began to care for the traveling and the needy. Gradually, "hospitality" morphed into fancy dinner parties and having a beautiful home to entertain guests.

> *There is something amazingly beautiful about sharing a meal around your table.*

In our Western culture there has been another shift over the past few years. We've become accustomed to taking people out to dinner or out for coffee and putting them up in hotels. Now, I'm not saying that hotels are bad at all. Trust me, I've stayed in my fair share of hotels, and I have enjoyed the peace and quiet, particularly when getting ready to speak. However, what I am saying is that perhaps we've missed the joy of inviting others into both our hearts and our homes. There is something amazingly beautiful about sharing a meal around your table.

I'll never forget traveling to Poland to speak several years ago. I was traveling alone. My hostess, Alina, invited me and offered me what they had termed "the prophet's room." She and her husband decided when they built their house that they would always have a room set aside to host traveling speakers. The space was lovely and quiet, fresh and clean. It was the perfect space to sleep and the perfect place to pray and prepare for my meetings. My hosts allowed me plenty of time to get ready and they also entertained me with delicious food, coffee, and conversation. Now, I don't always stay in homes when I travel and speak. I have some pet allergies, so often a hotel is a better choice for me. However, I had a lovely and restful time in Alina's house.

OPEN YOUR HOME

I learned about a woman in Ukraine named Olga. She is a leader in her church and has discipled many other female leaders and Bible study teachers. Olga used her home, especially in the early days of the war with Russia, to take in other Bible study leaders and their families who were fleeing the country. Olga's home became a safe resting place as many made their way out of the country. At one point, Olga had at least three families staying with her until they could find safe passage. Though food supplies were running low, Olga shared what she had and prayed over each family as they moved to escape the horror of the war. What a beautiful example of someone who had an open-door policy to be used by God.

Over the years, I've asked God to use my home for His glory. I used to love to take women out for coffee. Sometimes I still do. However, in the past couple of years, I've started inviting women into my home for coffee and prayer. It has been such a delight to open my home and open my ears for how I might best encourage and pray. Women who come to pray with me seem to be more relaxed opening their hearts in my home rather than in a coffee shop.

OPEN YOUR HEART

Ultimately, Christian hospitality is more than inviting people into our homes. It's opening your heart to new and stronger relationships. It's welcoming the poor and the broken, as well as your close friends. It's rooted in the understanding that everyone has a seat at God's table.

One of the most important steps in moving from loneliness to having solid friendships is having an open heart. Too often women build walls around their hearts because of past hurt. Those walls, while designed to protect our hearts, end up damaging our hearts. We don't enjoy deep intimate relationships because we don't feel like we can trust our hearts to others. However, Paul exhorted us to "welcome one another" (Rom. 15:7 ESV).

JESUS' THOUGHTS ON HOSPITALITY

Jesus took hospitality to another level. He gave guidelines for banquet-hosting and instructed His followers to invite not only their friends, but also "the poor, the crippled, the lame, and the blind" (Luke 14:12–24). He continued that doing so will be a blessing, in part because these guests would not be able to repay the host.

When we welcome the broken, the poor, the messy, and the marginalized, we welcome Him.

One time Jesus was teaching His disciples about what it will be like when the Son of Man comes again. He described a scene where all people from all nations are before Him, and King Jesus invites some to enter heaven saying, "For I was hungry and you gave me something to eat, I was thirsty and you gave me something to drink, I was a stranger and you invited me in, I needed clothes and you clothed me, I was sick and you looked after me, I was in prison and you came to visit me" (Matt. 25:35–36). Jesus was teaching us to see His image in humanity, in the broken, the poor, the messy, and the marginalized. When we welcome them, we welcome Him.

Throughout the New Testament, hospitality generally referred to caring for strangers or other Christians in need of assistance. Shared meals were common. People knocking on your door with no place to stay was an opportunity to follow Christ's command and host people for the night. It was not considered optional for those who followed Christ—it was the norm.

If we want to move past our loneliness and cultivate deeper connections, we need to get back to the idea of hospitality. We are called to welcome others.

A WELCOMING HOME, NOT A "PERFECT" ONE

Home is to be a wonderful place where family members feel safe and friends feel welcomed. One way to do this is to create intentional spaces for people to gather and have conversation. Perhaps it's a central table where you invite people in to enjoy a meal. Often our temptation is to avoid inviting others into our home unless it looks perfect. But that's never been the goal of hospitality.

As I mentioned earlier in the book, Steve and I served in Khartoum, Sudan, for a couple of years back in the 1980s. When we were learning about the culture, we learned that in that region, the Middle East/North Africa, hospitality is everything. If someone comes unexpectedly to knock at your door, you *never* leave them standing out there. You invite them in for coffee or tea or whatever you have. At the time I had a toddler and never quite knew what condition the house would be in when folks stopped by. I wanted my home to be neat and tidy before I allowed others to enter. However, I learned quickly that I had to adjust my attitude and embrace the culture. I loved hospitality when it was planned, but it definitely took some adjusting on my part when hospitality was spontaneous! It took me a while to learn that there's a definite difference between entertaining and hospitality.

I read this quote recently, and I feel it's accurate on the difference between entertainment and hospitality. Entertainment declares, however subtly, "This is a show. My house is on show for you and my possessions are on display for you to admire and be entertained by." Hospitality on the other hand whispers, "What's mine is yours."[3] Come in, feel welcomed, and let's connect.

At times, the challenge is figuring out how to create a home that welcomes others, where you take care of the things in your home without allowing them to become idols. I have wrestled with this question particularly when I was raising my kids. All our kids played soccer for a while, so it was not uncommon for soccer balls to be flying through the house. I never bought expensive lamps or other items because I didn't want to worry about them breaking. I also didn't want to be too anxious over furniture getting ruined.

On the other hand, I wanted to teach my children to respect the homes of others and the value of the furnishings in them. It helped me tremendously to remember the reason I bought the items in the first place. What do I mean? If I purchased a table, the purpose was for friends and family to gather around the table to eat and enjoy conversation. When I purchased a couch, its purpose was for friends and family to gather on the couch to chat or watch a movie or read a book or simply cuddle. After reflecting on this, I decided that in our house the kids would eat at the table and the couch would be for reading, cuddling, watching TV, or simply having conversation. Remembering why I bought things in the first place helped me. And to be honest, my husband, Steve, hated sticky things or ground up food in the couch, so that also helped my decision!

For you, it might be different. You might have purchased your couch for eating or for other activities. Each person's reasons for the things in their homes might vary. The important thing is for you to create safe spaces for friends and family to feel welcome and for you and your spouse to agree together on what works best for your family. Give intentional thought to what will make people feel welcome.

Gathering at the Dinner Table as a Place of Connecting

I recently had a conversation with a friend who told me that she and her husband bought a long, roomy table because they want to have others in their home for meals. They desired a gathering place that could host many. What a great reason to buy a large table!

The table is central as a place of connecting throughout the Scriptures. Jesus Himself invites us and welcomes us to His table. I attend a church where we serve Communion at the end of every service. It is such a precious sacrament to me. As I watch people go down front to receive Communion, I am reminded not only of the price Jesus paid to welcome all to His table; every time I take Communion, I am reminded that the Lord invites, "Come, you are welcome! You have a seat at My table." As we look toward the future, we see the marriage supper of the Lamb. What a beautiful example of hospitality.

In your home, use your table as a place to gather, enjoy, and connect. Celebrate dinner time with your family but go beyond and invite your friends and neighbors to join. When new people arrive at your church, invite them over. During the holidays, look for those who are lonely to invite to your table. As they enjoy delicious food, they can enjoy delightful conversations.

A few years ago, a couple of our adult kids hosted "Big Table" dinner parties. They invited people from all walks of life. They served a bunch of delicious food, opened in prayer, and then just enjoyed getting to know people through conversation and games. The feedback was astounding! Many people had not been invited to big dinner parties like that and they immediately felt more connected with others. Several commented, "We've been longing for community, and we've never experienced anything like this!"

Friend, the world is a lonely place. Invite people in. Gather them around your table and make them feel welcome.

Starting a Small Group in Your Home

Another way to welcome others is to start a small group in your home where you can have safe discussions about the Bible and where you can share prayer requests. Community groups are one of the best vehicles I know to disciple folks. The early church used their homes for this purpose.

One of my friends started a community group with her neighbors in her home to study a book written about anxiety and contentment.[4] It became a wonderful place for her to invite her unbelieving friends and, as a result, many came to Christ.

Neighboring Well in Our Polarized World

In one of the churches we pastored, a group of clergy from our area went to the town's government officials and asked what the churches could do to help some of the social issues our area was facing. After a bit of thought the town officials came back and said, "Teach your people to be good neighbors." It was a rather astounding statement! Christians were no better at neighboring than those who didn't follow Jesus!

> We need to consider something: Are we Christians known for being loving or are we known for shouting about our opinions?

After that meeting, we looked for some folks who would be willing to throw a block party in their neighborhood. Our church leadership offered $100.00 to each host or block party committee to help with the costs. The goal? Just love on your neighbors. The results were fantastic! Friend, Jesus calls us to be good neighbors even to those who have differing political or religious views.

Jesus told a story in the gospel of Luke to illustrate what neighboring looks like when people are polarized. Jesus told a story in response to a question lobbed at him by an expert in the law, "Teacher, what must I do to inherit eternal life?" In response Jesus told a story (Luke 10:25–37). In Jesus' story a man was robbed and beaten up on the way to Jericho. Two religious leaders, a priest and a Levite, who also happened to be traveling on the road, passed by the wounded man and did nothing. Then a Samaritan man saw the wounded man, took pity on him, cleaned his wounds, took him to an inn, and paid for him to stay. Now, Samaritans had different theological and cultural views than the Jews. It's interesting that in Jesus' story, two very prominent religious leaders would have nothing to do with the Samaritan. It seems to me that there are some parallels between this story and our culture today.

We need to consider something: Are we Christians known for being loving or are we known for shouting about our opinions? What's the point of Jesus' story? Let me remind you, those around us often have opposing views about this or that, and yet we are called to love like Jesus and be neighborly. Don't just invite your friends over. Seek to invite others in who have very different views than you do.

Welcoming Others into Your Friend Circles

One of the most significant ways we can welcome others is by inviting them into our friend circles. At times, even as believers, we can be a bit cliquey. We have our friend group, or our small group, and we are content to just have those few. I'm not saying you have to be friends with everyone (we've already covered that), but we do have to be welcoming. Who is new in your church or neighborhood who you might include in your next gathering? I am convinced that most people are dying to feel invited and included.

Everyone has a story. Ask about their story and stay curious as they tell you their story. Offer the gift of your unhurried, full presence. Like Melodie at the beginning of this chapter discovered, it is hard to move into a new community. Plus, Melodie was carrying a heavy backstory. Praise God for the women who circled around her, welcomed her, and listened to her story. You can offer the same.

Slow Down to Be Welcoming

I'm mentioning it again because I feel one of the leading causes of our loneliness is the pace of our lives. We can't be welcoming without slowing down, and that's where the rub comes for many of us. I realize that I am often in a rush. I was born to go fast. However, over the last couple of years, I've really been praying about this because I am convinced that it hinders my ability to be welcoming like Jesus. In light of this, I've started putting some small practices into place. And I might add, I have a lot further to go in this area. One thing I've been experimenting with has

I'm trying to remember to walk slowly so that I can stop and say hi to people.

been slowing down when I'm pulling out of my driveway to stop and talk with my neighbors.

Another simple practice when I order coffee at Starbucks is to ask the barista how they are doing and truly pause for a few minutes to listen. When I feel the angst of hurry creeping in and I'm in the grocery store, I'll purposely choose the longest line to practice slowing down. All these practices may sound simple to you, but to me they are a challenge. They may seem unrelated to hospitality to you, but nothing is further from the truth. Remember, hospitality is making others feel welcomed. If you are always in a rush, no one will feel welcomed.

Several years ago, I attended a conference to get my John Maxwell leadership certification. In part of our training, John told us to learn to "walk slowly through the room." At the time, I wondered to myself if John himself really practiced that. The next morning, I went to the restroom during the first session. Everyone else was already in the meeting room getting ready for session two. As I was walking back to the meeting, John and his event planner were together in the hall. Even though John was to take the stage in a few minutes, he stopped. He welcomed me, asked my name, and wanted to know if I was enjoying the event. I never forgot that two-minute interaction. I felt so welcomed.

I've taken it as a personal lesson and am trying to remember to walk slowly through the halls of church on Sunday, to walk slowly through my neighborhood, to walk slowly through an event I am speaking at so that I can stop and say hi to people and so others will feel welcomed by me. You never know who you might meet along the way who is feeling lonely or disconnected.

HOSPITALITY IS A FORM OF DISCIPLESHIP

Ultimately, learning to offer hospitality is part of our discipleship. As Rosaria Butterfield titled her fine book, the gospel comes with a house key.[5] Jesus invites everyone to His table. All are welcome. I think in the past we have rationalized hospitality as something only perfectly organized and designed owners of HGTV-ready homes can do. But as followers of Jesus, all of us are to be practicing hospitality! God wants us to demonstrate His heart to the world by inviting others in and making them feel welcome.

> *Lord Jesus, thank You for the hospitality You continually offer me. Thank You for inviting me to Your table to enjoy communion with You. Lord, as I think about Your heart for the world, I pray that You would help me to open my heart and my home to others. I pray that I would welcome others as You do. I pray that my home would be a place where others are healed from their loneliness and where they experience the love of Christ through me. Thank You that as I seek to ease the loneliness of others, You ease mine.*

DIGGING DEEPER
INTO CONNECTION

Deeper Connection with God

1. Look up the following verses and consider what they teach you about God's heart for hospitality.

   Isaiah 58:7
   Mark 9:37
   1 Timothy 5:10
   1 Peter 4:8–9

   Why do you think hospitality is so important to God?

2. From your perspective, how might opening your heart and your home ease not only the loneliness of others, but also your own loneliness?

3. If you took Jesus' words about inviting the "poor, the crippled, the lame, and the blind" seriously when you host a luncheon or dinner, how might your relationships change?

Deeper Connection with Yourself

1. What most often prevents you from opening your home to others?

2. What might be some practices you could put in place to become more comfortable with hospitality?

Deeper Connection with Others

1. Instead of meeting a friend at a coffee shop, invite her to your house this week for coffee. Ask about her story and then spend time praying together.

2. Host a "Charcuterie and Conversation" evening with a few of your friends. Lead a conversation around the idea of hospitality. Have your friends share tips on what makes hospitality easier for them.

God Welcomes You

"While they were eating, Jesus took bread, and when he had given thanks, he broke it and gave it to his disciples, saying, 'Take it; this is my body.' Then he took a cup, and when he had given thanks, he gave it to them, and they all drank from it. 'This is my blood of the covenant, which is poured out for many'" (Mark 14:22–24a).

"But the crowds learned about it and followed him. He welcomed them and spoke of God, and healed those who needed healing" (Luke 9:11).

"And if I go and prepare a place for you, I will come back and take you to be with me that you also may be where I am" (John 14:3).

"Let us then approach God's throne of grace with confidence, so that we may receive mercy and find grace to help us in our time of need" (Heb. 4:16).

KARLA AND JOANN'S STORY

Karla was with many of her closest friends for a conference. This event was a great opportunity to be with like-minded women, hear the Word, and grow in her faith. She was surrounded by hundreds of Christian women and looked forward to meeting as many as possible.

This event was designed to have deep sessions and some free time to reflect, pray, or get together in a group and discuss the topic at hand. Her personal favorite time was joining women to talk and pray. Every break she had, she tried to join a different group of women just to connect. God was moving in amazing ways. However, without realizing it, Karla had offended Joann.

Joann was hurt that Karla didn't have more time for her. She thought that when Karla was going from group to group that she was intentionally ignoring her. As a result, Joann went silent. It wasn't until months later that Karla figured out why her friend had ghosted her.

Months after the conference, Karla heard from a mutual friend that she had hurt Joann. Karla took initiative and apologized, clarifying that was never her intention. She was simply trying to connect with people and enjoy the conference. However, Joann had taken offense, and along with that offense had constructed a narrative in her mind. Her narrative told her that Karla no longer wanted to be friends.

It wasn't until years later that Joann finally realized she had given up a dear friend over a silly offense. She took initiative, contacted Karla, apologized, and asked if they could start over. With tears and forgiveness, the two women reignited their friendship.

CHAPTER NINE

Don't Be Easily Offended

Forgive one another.

COLOSSIANS 3:13

To love at all is to be vulnerable. Love anything, and your heart will certainly be wrung and possibly broken. If you want to make sure of keeping it intact, you must give your heart to no one, not even to an animal. Wrap it carefully round with hobbies and little luxuries; avoid all entanglements; lock it up safe in the casket or coffin of your selfishness. But in that casket—safe, dark, motionless, airless— it will change. It will not be broken, it will become unbreakable, impenetrable, irredeemable.

C. S. LEWIS

I remember the conversation so well. I was a teenager and taking a walk with a mentor who did campus ministry at my high school. As we walked, she told me, "Becky, you have a sensitive spirit. It's a gift from God. But you will have to be careful, or you will get your feelings hurt a lot and it will discourage you from the things God will call you to do." At the time, I felt a bit rebuked and discouraged. All through my childhood I'd heard from adults, "Why do you always have to cry? You're so sensitive! Stop crying."

Truthfully, I hated that part of myself. I couldn't figure out why it was so easy for me to cry, and I definitely couldn't figure out how to stop. I already felt frustrated with my sensitive nature, so when the mentor spoke to me about my being tender and at times touchy, I had a hard time not taking offense. However, I never forgot her words. As I went off to college, I carried her words with me and asked God to help me grow thicker skin.

God didn't change my personality. However, what He did do was gradually give me the grace to not become so easily offended. The ministry leader who challenged me in high school was absolutely correct. If I took offense easily, it would hinder the work God would eventually call me to do.

Every one of us will have hurtful and painful experiences in our lives as a result of those close to us. However, how we handle those experiences will either grow our ability to love others or diminish our ability to love. As author Francis Frangipane wrote, "Painful experiences are allowed by God to teach us how to love our enemies. Our character is tested by the way we respond and handle these experiences. If we still have unforgiveness toward someone, we have failed this test."[1] In addition, taking and hanging on to offense will ruin your relationships.

Every relationship will offer you an opportunity to take offense. Yes, there are injustices and may even be more serious offenses committed against us.

However, what is shocking is that it is often the small offenses that trip us up: the thoughtless word from a friend, the lunch forgotten, or the tiff over a difference of opinion. We latch on to those offenses and rehearse them in our heads, nurturing our hurt feelings and creating a monument to our own pain. Some of us take it a step further, creating stories in our heads, assuming we know the motives of the other. However, in the process, we forfeit close friendships.

The truth is when you take offense, you take Satan's bait. "The Greek word for offense is *skandalon*, from which we get the word scandal. It was originally the name of the part of a trap to which the bait is attached, hence the trap of snare itself."[2] Satan wants to isolate us, and he has no greater way to do this than tempting us to take offense.

WHAT DOES IT MEAN TO TAKE OFFENSE?

When you take offense, you hold on to hurt or anger over what someone else has said or done, and as a result, you regress emotionally. It's not just that you get annoyed. There are little annoyances that simply happen. Instead, you hang on to the hurt and pain rather than letting it go and offering the offender grace. As a result, you end up losing connection in your relationships. Wise Solomon from the Old Testament wrote, "Whoever would foster love covers over an offense, but whoever repeats the matter separates close friends" (Prov. 17:9). When you take offense, you repeat the hurt in your head over and over rather than letting it go. It becomes your narrative.

Paul wrote to the believers living in Colossae to "bear with each other and forgive one another if any of you has a grievance against someone. Forgive as the Lord forgave you" (Col. 3:13). The word for grievance in Greek is *memphomai*, which means a complaint against another.[3] It implies quarrels. This is important to understand because when we take offense it's usually over some quarrel or misunderstanding. Paul is not talking here about violent crimes or huge acts of betrayal, but personal problems between people.

We have many who are living lonely lives because they simply can't get past what someone said or did years ago. Certainly, this is true in the church. I remember hearing about two pastors who had had a disagreement years before and, as a result of that disagreement, refused to ever be on the same platform together. How sad! It would have been such a great testimony for Christ if they had been able to look beyond their differences and model for the church the unity of Christ.

Can I just be so bold as to say, we've *all* been hurt by churches? I'm not trying to be unempathetic, it's just that everyone I know has been hurt at some point. It makes sense because the body of Christ is made up of broken people. We hurt each other. Hopefully, we apologize and reconcile. However, this I know: God doesn't give us permission to drop out of His body or to hold grudges. We are part of the family of Christ, and I don't see any evidence that biblically supports cutting off the family. It's tough. I know. I've been hurt countless times by various churches. However, I've learned to let it go, understanding that people are human, and they likely didn't even know they hurt me, just as I'm unaware of times I've been the one who was hurtful.

Let me take a moment and clarify that for the purposes of this chapter, we're talking about hurt feelings, being falsely accused, disagreements, misunderstandings, and the like. Those are offenses.* However, people often treat offenses as though they're criminal. On a scale of one to ten, with one being a minor issue and ten being a horrific crime, everything becomes a ten to the

---

* Many people experience more egregious circumstances that are difficult to work through, and if that is your situation, know I grieve with you. And I encourage you to seek professional counseling or even to involve law enforcement if that is called for.

person who is easily offended. As a result, they put distance in the relationship or cut off the relationship entirely, only to discover that they are living a lonely life.

WHAT DOES JESUS SAY ABOUT OFFENSE?

Jesus had some hard words about not taking offense and offering grace instead. In His amazing Sermon on the Mount where He instructed His listeners in what it meant to follow Him, He said, "For if you forgive other people when they sin against you, your heavenly Father will also forgive you. But if you do not forgive others their sins, your Father will not forgive your sins" (Matt. 6:14–15). Whoa! That's a strong statement! Friends, Jesus took forgiving others very seriously. It's not optional depending on where you are on your spiritual journey. It's mandatory!

As I've considered why Jesus was so firm on this topic, I've come to realize that we really can't enjoy Christ's forgiveness unless we allow it to flow through our lives to others. The forgiveness Jesus extends is meant to set us free, but some of us are still in bondage to our offender. When we take offense, we nurture and stroke our hurt feelings or anger, and ultimately, we live trapped lives. Our unforgiveness keeps us in prison. We're left with countless arguments in our heads about why we're justified to be angry or hurt or whatever. The truth is, according to the gospel, our ongoing anger is not justified. We may feel initial anger over some injustice or slight done against us, but we are never justified in hanging on to our anger!

You might be wondering, "Well, isn't there a time to be angry?" Of course. But we must rely on the Holy Spirit to discern whether our anger is justified, and when it has occurred simply because our feelings are hurt. Righteous anger is in a different category, and it belongs to God, not us. Am I angry because the church no longer uses the hymnals my great-grandparents donated many decades ago? Or am I angry because rent for a neighborhood storefront unjustly shot up so high the long-time family-owned business was squeezed out? I love the way author and radio host Brant Hansen puts it: "We are too good at deceiving ourselves to know if we have 'righteous anger' or not."[4] Maybe you feel offended and honestly have good reason to. But here's the thing: I have searched Scripture from cover to cover and nowhere do I see us encouraged to hang on to anger or hurt. Instead, grace is to flow unhindered through the channels of our lives.

How do we change the narrative in our heads so that we don't become trapped, and we can enjoy the deep connections God delights to give us?

Think the Best of People—Not the Worst

It's amazing how often we assume the worst about others rather than the best. We take offense because someone forgot our birthday. We assume they don't value the relationship when in reality, they are overwhelmed with the chaos of their own lives. Or they just forgot, as we ourselves do. Or we might take offense when someone doesn't greet us at church. We assume the worst and imagine, "that person doesn't care about me." In reality, they might just be spacy and have a lot on their mind that morning.

Maybe you didn't get invited to a gathering and you assume that person has forgotten you or they have ostracized you because you're divorced or widowed. That might be the furthest thing from their minds! They might have gathered people who have similar interests. Assume the best. Later you can invite the person over for a cup of coffee and ask them about their story. Maybe you feel overlooked at work because you didn't receive the job promotion. You assume it is because you're quiet or you're too outspoken when in reality it might have nothing to do with that. Assume the best of your boss. They might be looking for a very specific skill set.

> **What do we do when we've already taken offense? Have a self-management meeting.**

Friend, when you feel yourself taking offense, stop. Change the narrative in your head and assume the best about the other person. Continually offer grace. Let it flow from your life like a river. Grace gives the other person the benefit of the doubt.

The question then becomes, what do we do when we've already taken offense? Rather than becoming trapped, how do we offer forgiveness, especially when people all around us disagree, annoy, or hurt us? We have a self-management meeting.

This is a principle I have taught in recent years to help people process some of the feelings that overwhelm them. We are called to be filled with the Spirit and for self-control to flow through our lives. At times we need a meeting between us and the Holy Spirit where we can reflect on our attitudes and clarify where our faulty thinking lies. In a self-management meeting, no one else is invited except you and the Holy Spirit. You ask yourself some penetrating questions and invite the Holy Spirit to search your heart and bring conviction.

Are you ready to have a self-management meeting?

Great. Here are five questions to get you started.

FIVE QUESTIONS TO ASK YOURSELF NEXT TIME YOU'VE TAKEN OFFENSE

1. How is holding on to my hurt or grudge helping me? (Col. 3:13) When I ask myself this question, I begin to realize that hanging on to hurt or anger does nothing to benefit me in any way. Quite the opposite: it makes me anxious and unsettled. It gives me high blood pressure and heartburn. And it destroys relationships.

I believe that one of the key contributing factors to our current epidemic of loneliness is our inability to forgive freely. As a result, we have mothers and daughters not speaking, siblings who haven't talked for years, neighbors and friends who are distanced, and members of churches who are repeatedly leaving because of church hurt. The answer is to let go. Your anger is not helping you. To the contrary, it is pushing others away. If you're living a lonely life, perhaps start by asking yourself if you are holding on to hurt from some past offense.

2. What can I take responsibility for? (Prov. 28:13) When I have been hurt or misunderstood in my relationships, I need to ask the Holy Spirit to probe my heart and show me what I can take responsibility for. When I do this, I begin to realize that perhaps I didn't communicate well. Or it could be that I overreacted to some insignificant comment. Maybe the other person was simply having a bad day and I took what they said too seriously. Or possibly that person felt misunderstood by something I said or did. I might have failed to be sensitive to what they were feeling. Or is it conceivable that I triggered defensiveness in the other person by coming on too strong with my own opinions?

The point is, if I analyze the offense I've taken, and ask the Holy Spirit to show me what I can take responsibility for, He is faithful to show me. This helps in two ways. First, I can offer an apology. Second, I can offer grace to the other person, realizing that neither of us are perfect. All of us make mistakes in relationships. At the end of the day, I can choose to praise God for another opportunity to offer grace.

3. How do I need to change as I move forward? (Matt. 7:5) Jesus said we were to take the plank out of our own eye before we attempted doing eye surgery on someone else. What did He mean? Often, we take offense and judge the other person for offending us. Rather than finding something wrong with them, Jesus counsels us to consider what's wrong with us first.

When we take offense, we need to look internally and spend some time reflecting on what caused us to take offense. Were we hurt? Insulted? Did we feel devalued? Excluded? By analyzing what we felt, we are able to figure out how to move forward.

For example, if we felt devalued, we can spend some time remembering that God values us deeply. He calls us chosen, holy, and dearly loved (Col. 3:12). If we felt taken advantage of, we might need to consider better boundaries moving forward.

4. Do I value this relationship? (1 Peter 4:8) I love the way Peter wrote, "Above all, love each other deeply, because love covers over a multitude of sins." Friend, relationships are precious! They take work but they are worth the effort. Pausing to consider, "How much do I value this relationship?" will help you clarify quickly what offenses to let go.

Now to be clear, you can't cultivate deep connections with thousands of people. Our humanity limits us. However, if you've been close friends for years, or if you have a misunderstanding with a close family member, in the words of Solomon, "Go—to the point of exhaustion" and apologize (Prov. 6:3). Take the lead to work things out. Why? Because your relationships are precious. Express how much you value the relationship to the other person.

5. How do I want to show up to initiate restoration? (Matt. 5:9) Jesus said, "Blessed are the peacemakers." To be a peacemaker is to initiate reconciliation where possible. Within your community or close friend group, where relationships have become fractured or distant, take initiative. Consider what you have to do to open the conversation so that your relationship can be healed.

When our relationship with God was broken by our sin, He took the initiative by sending Jesus. Christ Himself went to extreme measures to provide reconciliation. He wasn't defensive, though He certainly could have been. When Jesus went to the extreme for us, how can we then hold a grudge against those who hurt us? Letting it go and seeking reconciliation could be the answer to your loneliness.

The questions above can feel a bit overwhelming. As you finish reflecting, why don't you take this moment to pray?

Lord Jesus, I realize so often I am easily offended. Examine my heart, Holy Spirit, show me where I have assumed the worst about people or taken their comments personally, where I have nurtured my hurt feelings instead of letting them go. Lord, cleanse me, I pray. Help me, through the power of Your Spirit, to think the best of people, and when

I feel tempted to take offense, help me instead to let it go. I pray that grace would flow out of my life today so that You are honored and others feel safe with me.

DIGGING DEEPER INTO CONNECTION

Deeper Connection with God

Read Matthew 18:21–35, the parable of the unmerciful servant. Spend a few minutes quietly reflecting on the story and its application to your life. What do you feel God is inviting you to do?

Deeper Connection with Yourself

1. *On a scale of 1–10, 1 being not at all to 10 being highly sensitive, how sensitive would you say you are?*

2. *Have you put distance in any relationships because you've been offended? How has doing so enabled you to hold on to that offense?*

3. *How might you experience less loneliness by letting it go?*

Deeper Connection with Others

1. *Ask three people close to you, "Do you think I get easily offended?" No matter how they answer, simply thank*

them for their feedback. Then take their answers to the
Lord in prayer and ask Him to help you to develop a loving spirit that is not easily offended.

2. Spend a few moments in prayer, asking the Holy Spirit
to search your heart. Ask Him to reveal any of your
relationships where there is tension. Then set up a time to
meet with the person who's in that relationship with you
and ask them how you could improve the connection between the two of you. Listen without becoming defensive,
and then tell them how much you value their feedback.

God Is Forgiving—He Doesn't Hold on to Offenses

*"For as high as the heavens are above the earth, so great is his love
for those who fear him; as far as the east is from the west, so far
has he removed our transgressions from us"* (Ps. 103:11–12).

*"Who is a God like you, who pardons sin and forgives the
transgression of the remnant of his inheritance? You do not stay
angry forever but delight to show mercy. You will again have
compassion on us; you will tread our sins underfoot and hurl all
our iniquities into the depths of the sea"* (Mic. 7:18–19).

*"All the prophets testify about him that everyone who believes in
him receives forgiveness of sins through his name"* (Acts 10:43).

"In him we have redemption through his blood, the forgiveness of sins, in accordance with the riches of God's grace that he lavished on us" (Eph. 1:7–8a).

"Forgive as the Lord forgave you" (Col. 3:13b).

"If we confess our sins, he is faithful and just and will forgive us our sins and purify us from all unrighteousness" (1 John 1:9).

MISSY'S STORY

Missy has spent the majority of her life in a wheelchair. Yet, she is one of the most joy-filled people I know. I asked her if she ever felt lonely. She wrote:

"Being wheelchair-bound felt somewhat lonely and isolating at times. When friendships failed, I wondered, Were we only friends because they felt sorry for me? In those moments, loneliness began to creep in, and I felt that no one knows what my daily challenges are like. As I'm getting older, I don't allow self-pity. It's not about the quantity of friends that I have in my life, but about the quality of those relationships.

"God has placed some wonderful people in my life who have encouraged me, despite how I appear on the outside. They see me for who God has created me to be. You may wonder how I have been able to overcome feelings of loneliness and isolation. It has not been easy. Just like anything else, this takes practice and hard work to accomplish. When I begin to sense loneliness coming, I immediately remember who my greatest friend is . . . God! Once I focus on all that He is to me, He begins to wipe away lonely feelings.

"Several years ago, I began texting prayers to my friends. God has given me a special gift, encouragement, and when I encourage and bless others, it comes back to me. I made the choice to use the gifts God has given me to cultivate community with others. I never will know the impact I may have on someone, and I may be just who they need in their times of trouble. As I take initiative and reach out with prayer, the other person is blessed, and my own loneliness is healed."

CHAPTER TEN

Find Your Prayer People

Carry each other's burdens,
and in this way you will fulfill the law of Christ.

Galatians 6:2

A company of praying people is a company of people equally
dependent on God. But we also come to prayer with equally good
help. The most eloquent spiritual giant and the most timid new
believer can pray boldly together because Jesus prays for them both.

Megan Hill

Early morning text message exchange:

> Me: Are you up? Wanna pray?
> Judy: Yes, let me grab coffee!

My friend Judy and I often exchange these early morning text messages. We're both early risers. So if a message comes in at 5:00 a.m., that's fine. Especially if it's an invitation to pray.

Judy and I have been praying together for years. I met her in one of the churches that my husband pastored in upstate New York. At the time, her girls were close in age to my two youngest, and Judy and I hit it off as friends. We both loved coffee, mothering, and ministry. More importantly, we both had a heart for prayer. We started praying for each other, our husbands, and our kids. Judy left upstate New York and moved to China, and then on to Michigan. Steve and I left upstate New York and moved to California, but Judy and I continued praying for each other. In 2005 we both moved to Colorado, and our in-person coffee and prayer times resumed. At times we pray in person, and sometimes we pray over the phone. Either way, our times before the Father are precious.

Now, it's many years later, and our kids are grown and married. We've got a mob of grandkids between us. But we continue to pray. As I look back over all the times we prayed Scripture over each other, over our spouses, over our kids and their future spouses, over our grandkids, over different ministries we've been involved with, my heart is overwhelmed. Judy and I have ugly cried together and shared openly about our struggles. We've hiked together and spent time praising God out loud as we've overlooked the mountains. We've celebrated each other's joys and grieved each other's sorrows. But at the root of it all has been our amazing prayer times. I'm astounded not only at the faithfulness of God through the years, but also at the devotion of a precious friend. What a gift to journey through life praying for my dear friend and knowing that she is covering me as well. I leave our times together feeling known, loved, and encouraged.

One of the best ways I know to become deeply bonded to others is by praying together. This is why praying together is so often recommended for marriage partners. When we pray with others, the Holy Spirit not only aligns our hearts with His, but He gives us loyal love for the other person. As a result, our relationship grows and we experience far less loneliness.

CARRY EACH OTHER'S BURDENS

You were never meant to carry your burdens alone. Paul wisely advised us that we are to "carry each other's burdens" (Gal. 6:2). The idea behind that word *burden* is a "weight that is heavy or crushing."[1] Our problems often feel heavy and crushing. Paul was suggesting that as we live in community with one another, we support and encourage one another in life's difficulties. This doesn't mean we try to fix other people's problems. Paul is not suggesting here that we don't exercise healthy boundaries. A friend of mine once said, "Boundaries make good neighbors," and I would add to that, boundaries make good friends. So then, what exactly does it mean to carry each other's burdens?

This is best illustrated with the story of a few great friends. One day Jesus was teaching in the village of Capernaum. A large crowd had gathered to hear him in a tiny house. People stood shoulder to shoulder trying to get a glimpse and hear a word from the Rabbi. However, all of a sudden in the middle of Jesus' teaching, the crowd heard digging on the roof. Clumps of thatch, dried mud, and straw began falling into the crowd, maybe sticking in people's hair! Gradually a stretcher was let down through the hole and, kerplunk! Right in front of Jesus. The Master must have smiled and perhaps even chuckled (Mark 2:1–12).

Some very dedicated friends had surrounded their friend who was paralyzed and carried him to Jesus, hoping that the miracle worker would heal. It took a

> *I'm guessing he had a big party with his friends that night!*

whole lot of courage and work to cut a hole in someone's roof, not to mention risking annoyance or anger from the crowd who was listening. Yet, these men were dedicated to their friend.

I've often wondered about the man who was paralyzed. He must have been extraordinary because often people with special needs in the time of Jesus were shunned. Many adopted a "victim" mentality. But this paralyzed man had obviously invested so much in his friendships that his friends willingly helped him. I'm guessing he changed his internal narrative from victim to victor. I imagine as his buddies came up with this outrageous plan to let him down through the roof the paralyzed man was smiling, perhaps saying, "Yes! I'm all in for the adventure!" If you read the entire story as recorded in Mark 2, you discover that Jesus forgave the paralytic's sins and then went on to heal him. The paralytic got up and walked out. I'm guessing he had a big party with his friends that night! What great friends this guy had!

When I think of this paralyzed man my thoughts go to my friend Missy, whose story I included right before this chapter. Missy's spina bifida doesn't hold her back. She is remarkable. I've never heard her complain, and she is an amazing friend to so many. If someone were to suggest to Missy that they let her down through the roof, she would immediately say, "I'm all in!" She's traveled overseas with Compassion International and doesn't hesitate to lift others up and help carry their burdens. In fact, as I write this, I just received an encouraging text from Missy letting me know she is praying for me.

PRAYER PARTNERS ARE STRETCHER BEARERS

While there are many ways to carry each other's burdens, the best way I know is to pray. In our friendships, we need to be "stretcher bearers" for one another to carry our friends' burdens to Jesus. Through the years, God has allowed me to have friends who I know will go to prayer on my behalf and who I pray for regularly.

Prayer is a powerful connector. When we dare to believe that God answers our prayers and we are willing to fight for our friends on our knees, God answers, the evil one is thwarted, and our friendship grows.

James, the brother of Jesus, wrote, "Therefore confess your sins to each other and pray for each other so that you may be healed. The prayer of a righteous person is powerful and effective" (James 5:16). When you translate this verse literally in the Greek it can read awkwardly. However, I love how one theologian put it, that the idea behind earnest prayer here is energy.[2] Effective prayer takes commitment and intentional energy on our part.

To be a friend who will faithfully carry the burdens of others to the Lord in prayer takes energy and faithfulness to continue. However, the beauty that emerges from friends who faithfully pray for each other is remarkable. In addition to the power that comes from our prayers for one another, there is a depth to our relationship that emerges.

When we pray with and for our friends, the Holy Spirit unifies our hearts in extraordinary ways. At times when people say they are lonely, I want to ask, "Who are you praying with and for regularly?" Why not take a risk and ask someone to be a prayer partner with you? As you engage and pray with and for each other, your relationship is going to grow.

WHAT DOES IT TAKE TO BE A PRAYER PARTNER?

Availability

In order to be a prayer partner, we need to be available. What does this mean? It might mean spending less time at work, or it might mean making fewer commitments so you can be faithful to the friends with whom you are most connected.

Here's what I know—if you are so busy that you're not available when your friends need prayer, you will lose the close connection. We definitely need boundaries around time with our spouses and families. However, I fear that in our present culture, instead of boundaries we've put up walls sending the signal, "Don't tell me your problems because I don't have time to listen and pray." Somehow, we need to quiet that internal hurry that we've become so addicted to and make ourselves available for our friends.

Vulnerability

A prayer partnership is not the same as mentorship. When two people are prayer partners they are on a level playing ground. Both need to choose to be vulnerable and both need to take initiative. When we're vulnerable with each other we expose our inner thoughts and feelings. There's risk involved. However, when we feel safe enough to share our struggles honestly with another human being, without the fear of rejection, our feelings of connectedness are strengthened. When another person offers us empathy rather than judgment, we feel a sense of belonging. Within the prayer partnership relationship, if you feel understood, you will take more risks in sharing your need for prayer. And, on the flip side, you offer more grace for your prayer partner to be vulnerable.

Confidentiality

One of the greatest ways to build a sense of safety in a prayer partnership is to be trustworthy about keeping confidences. We've all had people who offered to pray and then shared our stories with others. We felt hurt and exposed and reluctant to share again.

In a prayer partnership, I don't even share requests with my husband unless the other person gives permission. There are certain requests that are deeply personal, and I must be trusted to keep those requests confidential.

Intentionality

In order for prayer partnerships to be effective, there needs to be intentionality about praying together regularly. Judy, who I mentioned at the beginning of this chapter, is faithful at reaching out. Both our schedules are busy. We both travel, speak, and write. However, we are intentional about praying together. Intentionality includes answering text messages when either of us needs immediate prayer. I have been teaching at a conference and felt like I was under attack in some area of my walk. I have texted Judy in those moments and within minutes have received a reply that she is praying. Those quick text message exchanges remind me that I am not alone in the battle.

"HOW CAN I GET STARTED?"

In your friendships, look for people who take prayer seriously. You'll know them. They won't be hard to find because prayer permeates their lives. They will tell you they are praying for you, and they might ask how they can pray for you specifically. Ask God to show you those people. Then, ask them if they want to get together to pray. You can take a walk and pray together. Or you can have coffee and pray together. You can even pray together over the phone. My sister Lynne and her husband, Jim, pray with another couple over the phone every Sunday evening. They pray for their kids and grandkids. What a beautiful relationship they enjoy.

My in-laws, who have since passed away, used to pray every Sunday evening with several of their neighbors. At times through the years, I would forget and call them during the session. They'd pick up and then whisper, "Can't talk. We're praying. Love you." I loved that! What a blessing to know that my in-laws were dedicated to prayer partnerships.

As I reflect back on my life, my journey of marriage, raising kids, ministry life, writing life, and travel demands, I am thankful for the prayer partners who have journeyed with me. Judy is not my only prayer partner. I have Jill, Linda, Suzanne, Keri, Susie, Gayle, and others who faithfully pray for me and with me. They are my stretcher bearers. They celebrate the blessings with me and carry me before the Lord in the hard times. As a result, I rarely feel alone. I feel connected to them and tethered to the Lord in a way I can't even describe because my community helps me stay attached. It gives me a deep sense of belonging. However, beyond any human prayer partner I have enjoyed, there is One who is greater.

THE MOST FAITHFUL OF ALL PRAYER PARTNERS

When I consider prayer partners, the most amazing prayer partner hands down is Jesus Christ Himself. Paul wrote, "Christ Jesus who died—more than that, who was raised to life—is at the right hand of God and is also interceding for us" (Rom. 8:34). The writer of Hebrews echoes this thought, writing, "but because Jesus lives forever, he has a permanent priesthood. Therefore he is able to save completely those who come to God through him, because he always lives to intercede for them" (Heb. 7:24–25).

> **When you feel lonely, remind yourself—Jesus is praying for you.**

Think about that for just a moment. Day and night. While you work and while you sleep, Jesus Himself, who does not condemn you, is continually interceding for you. He allows no one to condemn you. He is your advocate, continually praying for you. What a prayer partner! Other prayer partners sleep, He does not. Other prayer partners cannot be available 24/7, but He is always available. Other prayer partners may grow weary, but He never does. Constantly you are being prayed for! What wonderful security that provides.

When you feel lonely, remind yourself—Jesus is praying for you. You are never alone or forgotten. You are seen and heard. No one can sever your connection to Christ. As He prays for you and you pray to Him, the Holy Spirit draws you into deeper union with Him. Your hearts are knit together. As you continue, over time, your loneliness will gradually be healed because you will realize you have the most secure connection with the King of kings. His desire is for you to know beyond a shadow of a doubt, you are never alone!

Oh Lord Jesus, I praise and thank You that You are my most faithful prayer partner. When I simply don't know what to pray, what a comfort that You Yourself are interceding for me before the Father. Thank You that Your commitment to me never wanes. Day and night You are interceding. I praise You that You have also given me the privilege of praying for others. What joy this brings to my life as I realize other believers are in the journey with me. As I pray for them, Your Holy Spirit reminds me that I am part of the extended body of Christ. Thank You for inviting me into the family where I belong and am surrounded with brothers and sisters in Christ who will pray with and for me. Thank You that I am always welcome in the throne room to lay my requests before you.

DIGGING DEEPER
INTO CONNECTION

Deeper Connection with God

1. Read Hebrews 4:16. What does it mean to you personally, that God invites you to enter into His presence with boldness and pray?

2. In addition to cultivating deeper connection with others when you pray for them, how does prayer help you connect more deeply with God?

3. Read Acts 4:23–31. The early church took praying together seriously. What can we learn from their example in this story?

Deeper Connection with Yourself

1. What keeps you from praying with others? How might it bring you deeper connection with others if you started praying together?

2. What have you learned about yourself after reading this book?

3. *In what ways do you need to change the narrative in your head and take more initiative to form deeper connections?*

4. *Which relationships in your life are most important to you? How will you connect with each person moving forward?*

5. *As you reflect back on this book, which chapter was most beneficial to you? What was your takeaway from that chapter?*

Deeper Connection with Others

1. *Plan to connect with three friends in this upcoming week. Call and set up a time to have lunch or get coffee or connect in a different way.*

2. *Take initiative to form a prayer partnership with at least one of your friends. Then, start gathering and praying together regularly.*

3. *Like Missy, whose story you read in this chapter, send a prayer text to at least three people letting them know you are praying for them.*

God Is the Perfect Prayer Partner

"The righteous cry out, and the LORD *hears them; he delivers them from all their troubles"* (Ps. 34:17).

"Call to me and I will answer you and tell you great and unsearchable things you do not know" (Jer. 33:3).

"Ask and it will be given to you; seek and you will find; knock and the door will be opened to you. For everyone who asks receives; the one who seeks finds; and to the one who knocks the door will be opened" (Matt. 7:7–8).

"Then Jesus told his disciples a parable to show them that they should always pray and not give up" (Luke 18:1).

A Few Final Thoughts

Thanks, friend, for journeying with me to cultivate deeper connections in a lonely world. When I started to write this book, I didn't realize the many shades of loneliness that people encounter. Those who are single feel lonely and wish they were married, while many feel lonely in their marriages. Others feel lonely because of walking through deep grief or having untruths told about them. Still others walk through loneliness because they've moved geographically. The truth is that feelings of isolation come in all shapes and sizes.

My prayer is that you've gained some practical tools to help you navigate those feelings and cultivate the type of deeper connections your heart longs to enjoy. Remember, God aches for you. He did everything possible to connect with you. When you feel lonely, remember, you are never alone because He is always with you.

Be intentional after finishing this book. Embrace humility in your friendships, offering to serve others and asking for help when you need it. Seek to be kind and let go of the tendency to criticize. Cultivate the beautiful quality of loyalty by contacting some of the friends that you've had for years. Take time to remember how precious they are to you. Stop comparing and don't become offended easily. If you find yourself tempted, quickly call a friend and ask her to pray for you. Practice being attentive in conversation and open both your heart and home to others. Have a friend over for coffee or invite a few people for dinner.

Just as you need deeper connections, so do others around you. Learn to offer comfort and be willing to receive comfort from others. Finally, find your prayer partners—your stretcher bearers. They're available, you just have to put the effort into finding them and inviting them to pray with you.

Before I say goodbye, why don't you set a goal of reaching out to three people each week for the next few months? Plan ahead some conversation starters like questions you might ask. Above all, spend time praying for those people and ask God to use you to bless them and that you will be blessed in return.

My prayers are with you as you seek to connect with others and live a less lonely life!

Acknowledgments

Writing a book is never a solo journey. It takes many to bring a book to life. I am so grateful for:

My husband, Steve. Thank you for your continued support and love and for making life fun!

My kids and kids-in-love:

Bethany and Chris, I am so thankful for the way the two of you live out the gospel every day in tangible ways. I love your heart for foster care and kids who have been traumatized and for the amazing parents you are to your five boys. I love you!

JJ and Shaina, I am so grateful for your commitment to Jesus, Compel Global, to the wounded, and to prayer. I love how you are raising your boys to trust Jesus and love others. I love you!

Stef and Dave, I'm grateful for your heart for the poor and broken, the messy and the marginalized. It's been fun to see you both grow in your careers and to see you thrive in your community. I am thankful for how deeply you love your kids and how deeply you love Jesus. I love you!

Keri and Zach, I'm thankful for your heart for worship, and for the Lord. It's been so fun to see your business, Bears Music Academy, grow. I love the way you both bring your strengths to your family and that you are raising your kids to love Jesus. I love you!

To my grandkids: I'm so thankful for each of you: Charlie, Ty, Josh, Selah, Zachary, Theo, Noah, Rayna, Cayden, Kinley, Tori, Melody, Asher, and Austin. I pray for each of you every day and am thrilled to see you growing up to love Jesus!

To my agent and trusted friend, Blythe Daniel. Thank you for your heart for this project and for always supporting me in prayer.

To all the men and women of Moody Publishers.

Judy Dunagan, my dear friend and acquisitions editor.

Pam Pugh, my amazing content editor. It has been so fun to work with you on this project! Thank you for your attention to detail!

All the other amazing people at Moody who help bring a book to life! Thank you, it is a privilege to be published by you.

To the faithful women who serve alongside me, Lynsey L'Ecuyer, Keri Spring, Gayle Call, Suzanne Kuhn . . . All of you are precious to me and I value your input in my ministry. I love each of you.

To all the women at New Life East, I love walking beside you in our journey of following Jesus.

Notes

CHAPTER 1: WHEN YOU DON'T FEEL CONNECTED

Epigraph: Daniel Goleman, *Social Intelligence: The New Science of Human Relationships*.

1. "New Surgeon General Advisory Raises Alarm About the Devasting Impact of the Epidemic of Loneliness and Isolation in the United States," US Department of Health and Human Services, May 3, 2023, https://www.hhs.gov/about/news/2023/05/03/new-surgeon-general-advisory-raises-alarm-about-devastating-impact-epidemic-loneliness-isolation-united-states.html.

2. Ruth Haley Barton, "The Loneliness of Leadership," Transforming Center, https://transformingcenter.org/2017/05/the-loneliness-of-leadership/.

3. Sherry Amatenstein, "Not So Social Media: How Social Media Increases Loneliness," *Psycom*, November 15, 2019, https://www.psycom.net/how-social-media-increases-loneliness.

4. Centers for Disease Control and Prevention, "Health Risks of Social Isolation and Loneliness," last reviewed March 20, 2023, https://www.cdc.gov/emotional-wellbeing/social-connectedness/loneliness.htm.

5. Ruth Myers, *The Perfect Love: Intensely Personal, Overflowing, Never Ending* (New York: Crown Publishing Group, 2011), 29.

6. Peter Scazzero, *Emotionally Healthy Relationships Day by Day* (Grand Rapids, MI: Zondervan, 2017), 12.

7. Based on article written by Dr. Tara Well, "Why Is Seeing Your Own Reflection So Important?," Psychology Today, August 5, 2018, https://www.psychologytoday.com/us/blog/the-clarity/201808/why-is-seeing-your-own-reflection-so-important.

CHAPTER 2: EMBRACE HUMILITY

1. Alice G. Walton, "Humble Friends to the Rescue," *The Atlantic*, February 18, 2012, https://www.theatlantic.com/health/archive/2012/02/humble-friends-to-the-rescue/252963/.

2. Andrew Arndt, *Streams in the Wasteland* (Colorado Springs: Navpress, 2022), 91–92.

3. Hayley Mullins and Erin Davis, *Living Out the One Anothers of Scripture: A 30-Day Devotional* (Niles, MI: Revive Our Hearts, 2020), 25.

4. Erika Allen, *ESV Prayer Journal: 30 Days on Humility* (Wheaton, IL: Crossway, 2022), Introduction.

5. Rowan Williams, *Where God Happens: Discovering Christ in One Another* (Boston: New Seeds, 2005), 130.

6. Pete Scazzero, "How Can Embracing Limits Make You a Better Leader?," https://www.youtube.com/watch?v=j8vCn_QZxGo.

7. Father Jeremy, "Prayer of the Heart and Humility," Orthodox Road: Rediscovering the Beauty of Ancient Christianity, January 19, 2014, https://www.orthodoxroad.com/prayer-heart-and-humility/.

8. Andrew Murray, *Humility* (Gainesville, FL: Bridge-Logos Publishers, 2000), quote from the front cover.

CHAPTER 3: LET GO OF A CRITICAL SPIRIT

Epigraph: Holley Gerth, *The Powerful Purpose of Introverts: Why the World Needs You to Be You.*

1. W. E. Vine, *An Expository Dictionary of New Testament Words* (Old Tappan, NJ: Fleming Revell, 1966), 292.

2. Posted on Instagram by Crystal Paine @themoneysavingmom.

3. Nelson Morais, "Speaker Says Compassion Will Win Over People," *Greenville Sun*, October 28, 2022, https://www.greenevillesun.com/news/local_news/hope-center-banquet-speaker-says-compassion-will-win-over-people/article_472862fa-563e-11ed-8224-079b9f9f00a6.html.

4. "Empathy," *Psychology Today*, http://www.psychologytoday.com/basics/empathy.

5. Becky Harling, *How to Listen So People Will Talk* (Minneapolis: Bethany House, 2017), 91.

CHAPTER 4: DEVELOP LOYALTY

Epigraph: Jennifer Dukes Lee, "This is the Church that Loyalty Built," July 1, 2013, https://jenniferdukeslee.com/this-is-the-church-that-loyalty-built/.

1. "The Story of Ruth in the Bible," BibleStudyTools.com, https://www.biblestudytools.com/bible-stories/story-of-ruth-in-the-bible.html.

CHAPTER 5: START CHEERING, STOP COMPARING

Epigraph: Jennie Allen, *Restless: Because You Were Made for More*.

1. *Merriam-Webster*, s.v. "envy (*n*.)," https://www.merriam-webster.com/dictionary/envy.

2. W. E. Vine, *An Expository Dictionary of New Testament Words* (Old Tappan, NJ: Fleming Revell, 1966), 37.

3. Katie M. Reid and Lee Nienhuis, "Real Talk About Friendship," *Martha & Mary Show*, June 15, 2022, https://www.katiemreid.com/martha-mary-show-podcast/.

4. "Giving Thanks Can Make You Happier," *Harvard Health Publishing*, August 14, 2021, https://www.health.harvard.edu/healthbeat/giving-thanks-can-make-you-happier.

5. Becky Harling, *Our Father: A Study of the Lord's Prayer* (Chicago: Moody Publishers, 2023).

CHAPTER 6: BE ATTENTIVE

Epigraph: Bob Goff, *Love Does: Discover a Secretly Incredible Life in an Ordinary World.*

1. Robert Kersherim, "Average Human Attention Span (by Age, Gender & Race)," Supportive Care ABA, October 5, 2023, https://www .supportivecareaba.com/statistics/average-attention-span#:~:text= The%20average%20attention%20span%20of,goldfish's%209%20 second%20attention%20span!

2. Emma Seppala, "What Is Your Phone Doing to Your Relationships?," *Greater Good Magazine*, October 10, 2017, https://greatergood .berkeley.edu/article/item/what_is_your_phone_doing_to_your_ relationships.

3. Gregory Jantz, *The Power of Connection* (Carol Stream, IL: Apsire Press/Tyndale House Ministries, 2022), 61, 64.

4. Jeremy Nobel, "Does Social Media Make You Lonely?," *Harvard Health Publishing*, December 21, 2018, https://www.health.harvard .edu/blog/is-a-steady-diet-of-social-media-unhealthy-2018122115600.

5. John Mark Comer, *The Ruthless Elimination of Hurry: How to Stay Emotionally Healthy and Spiritually Alive in the Chaos of the Modern World* (Colorado Springs: WaterBrook, 2019).

6. Becky Harling, *Psalms for the Anxious Heart: A 30-Day Devotional for Uncertain Times* (Chicago: Moody Publishers, 2020), 7.

7. Justin Zorn and Leigh Marz, "How Listening to Silence Changes Our Brains," *Time*, September 8, 2022, https://time.com/6210320/ how-listening-to-silence-changes-our-brains/.

8. Heather Holleman, *The Six Conversations: Pathways to Connecting in an Age of Isolation and Incivility* (Chicago: Moody Publishers, 2022), 24.

CHAPTER 7: OFFER AND RECEIVE COMFORT

Epigraph: Dee Brestin, *The Friendships of Women.*

1. Harrison Rainie, "The Buried Sounds of Children Crying," *US News & World Report*, May 1, 1995, 10.

2. W. E. Vine, *An Expository Dictionary of New Testament Words*, (Old Tappan, NJ: 1966), 207.
3. Ibid., 208. *Parakaleo* is the verb form of the noun *paraklesis*.
4. Sheon Han, "You Can Only Maintain So Many Close Friendships," *The Atlantic*, May 20, 2021, https://www.theatlantic.com/family/archive/2021/05/robin-dunbar-explains-circles-friendship-dunbars-number/618931/.
5. Dee Brestin, *The Friendships of Women: The Beauty and Power of God's Plan for Us* (Colorado Springs: David C. Cook, 2010), 108.
6. Danita Jenae, *How to Help Your Grieving Friend: The Companion's Guide*, 2021: a free downloadable gift on Danita's website, http://www.danitajenae.com.
7. Karen Mains, *Comforting One Another: In Life's Sorrows* (Nashville: Thomas Nelson, 1997), 23.

CHAPTER 8: OPEN YOUR HEART AND YOUR HOME

Epigraph: Rosaria Butterfield, *The Gospel Comes with a House Key*.
1. Dr. George Ross, "Hospitality in the New Testament," *Geaux Therefore*, May 3, 2021, https://www.nobts.edu/geauxtherefore/articles/2021/HospitalityNT.html.
2. "Julian the Apostate," in *New World Encyclopedia*, http://www.newworldencyclopedia.org/entry/Julian_the_Apostate, citing Charles Schmidt *The Social Results of Early Christianity* (London: Wm. Isbister, 1889), 328.
3. Karen Mains, *Open Heart, Open Home: The Hospitable Way to Make Others Feel Welcome and Wanted* (Wheaton, IL: Mainstay Church Resources, 1998), 30.
4. Linda Dillow, *Calm My Anxious Heart: A Woman's Guide to Finding Contentment* (Colorado Springs: NavPress, 2020).
5. Rosaria Butterfield, *The Gospel Comes with a House Key: Practicing Radically Ordinary Hospitality in Our Post-Christian World* (Wheaton, IL: Crossway, 2018).

CHAPTER 9: DON'T BE EASILY OFFENDED

Epigraph: C. S. Lewis, *The Four Loves*.

1. Francis Frangipane, *Strength For the Battle* (Lake Mary, FL: Charisma House, 2017), 98.
2. W. E. Vine, *An Expository Dictionary of New Testament Words* (Old Tappan, NJ: Revell, 1940), 131.
3. https://biblehub.com/lexicon/colossians/3-13.htm.
4. Brant Hansen, *Unoffendable: How Just One Change Can Make All of Life Better* (Nashville: Thomas Nelson, 2023), 64.

CHAPTER 10: FIND YOUR PRAYER PEOPLE

Epigraph: Megan Hill, *Praying Together*.

1. Rick Renner, "When To Help Bear Someone Else's Burden," Renner.org, May 23, 2023, https://renner.org/article/when-to-help-bear-someone-elses-burden/.
2. Jack W. Hayford, *New Spirit-Filled Life Bible* (Nashville: Thomas Nelson, 2014), 1657.

LISTEN TO MORE

On *The Connected Mom Podcast*, we have conversations about connecting more deeply with God, more empathetically with other moms, and more intentionally with your child.

SCAN THE CODE OR ACCESS ON
APPLE PODCASTS OR SPOTIFY

MORE BY BECKY HARLING

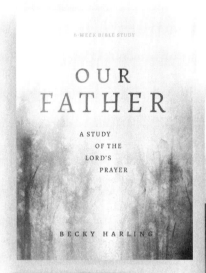

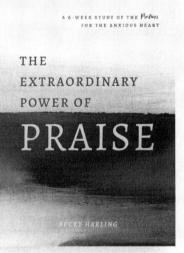

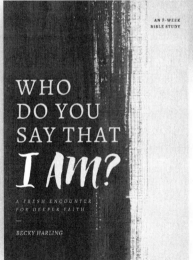

These accessible Bible studies by Becky Harling draw women deep into the Word for a true encounter with Christ, showing us the ways of praise, calmness, and courageous faith.

Also available as eBooks

FIND DAILY PEACE
IN A WORLD OF CHAOS

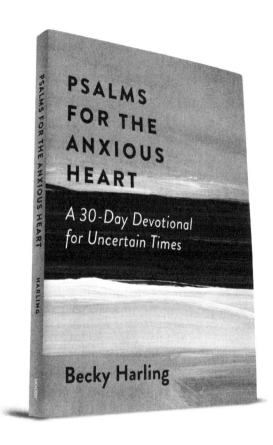

MOODY
Publishers®

*From the Word **to Life**®*

Psalms for the Anxious Heart is a short daily devotional that offers meditations of truth and peace. Each devotion includes a reading of a psalm, a brief teaching on the passage, a salient truth to cling to, and a suggested song to guide further meditation.

Also available as an eBook and audiobook